"Glenn has a true gift for taking things that are broken and fixing them. I sometimes call him the Mary Poppins of the workforce and now the rest of the world gets to learn exactly how he does it. This book is a roadmap for anyone who wants to affect change in their work center, empower teams, and grow as leaders. It's a must-read for every generation in the work-force."

Carrianne Ekberg, Executive Director for the Gig Harbor Downtown Waterfront Alliance and entrepreneur

"What I love about this book is how Glenn takes a practical and structured dynamic and connects it to the human element of emotion (energy in motion) and understanding. The weaving of his personal experience and insights touches upon relatable sentiments that allow the mind to explore these concepts from a centered space. Running a business and managing a team incorporates many moving parts and navigating the ebbs and flows of business, in my opinion, is more fulfilling when we have connection, understanding and joy within each aspect. The Human Centered Teams is a great guide toward creating that."

Dr Genie Markwell, Chiropractor and Entrepreneur

"The *Human Centered Team* is reflective of Glenn's style–a unique approach creating unique, genuine and deeply-rooted results. Glenn has the rare ability to quickly and sincerely connect with employees who typically can be more challenging to do so. By understanding and respecting the uniqueness of every person, he builds trustful and trusting relationship which can foster sincere and long-lasting organizational changes. He has shared in this book both his approach to this valuable work and also his life experiences that helped shape his philosophy which allows the reader to better understand the reasoning behind it."

Angie Feser, Parks Director City of Edmonds Washington

"Glenn Thank you for giving paths to learn and grow from your book, posts and when helping out businesses and cities you go to.

The most important thing that really hits me is what you start out with your mother and father, with some of us out there may have not had parents to mold us there are the ones that mentor us and help mold us in personal and work life to become who we are . Your book opens up to all that we can look back to those in our lives that changed us and made us want to be better and give to those around us to be help them become better.
Thank you very much Glenn..
All the best to you, you truly want to make a difference with the small things you do it is one person and one employee at a time."

Matthew Slater, Maintenance City of Kirkland Washington

"Having witnessed my father's journey from my own perspective, The Human Centered Team really brought me back to why Glenn developed this program and movement: To change the world through the workplace. Part self-help, part business and a very honest glimpse through key events from Glenn's life that called him to change and drove him to give others the same opportunity; The Human Centered Team is a call to be accountable for improving the lives of all the human beings that we have the privilege of working and communing with.

It was an emotional ride for me, and I uniquely understand how much more there is to the story. Everything in the book has many layers of depth, more to share, feel and experience. The Human Centered Team is just the beginning of a journey that many will take part in. My father's story, motivation and drive is authentic and beautiful because like his parents before him, he is truly inspired by service to others and humanity as a whole. His story just makes a greater message relatable."

Josh Akramoff, General Manager Akramoff LLC and Entrepreneur

The Human-Centered Team

Glenn Akramoff

For a copyright license, visit http://www.copyrightsnow.net/ or call toll free to copysupport@digi-rights.com. Cataloged in publication information is available from Library and Archives U.S.

E-book ISBN: 978-1-956257-67-0
Paperback ISBN: 978-1-956257-65-6
Hardback: ISBN: 978-1-956257-66-3

Formatting, publishing, cover design by Pierucci Publishing
Contributors: Dale Chaplin
Interior design by Sophie Hanks
Edited by Jonathan Richard Grant (JonathanRichardGrant.com)
Cover design by AJ McCormick

"Working with human beings to achieve more together
is what I love to do."

—*Glenn Akramoff*

Dedication

There would be no book, no movement, and no drive to create a better world without George and Louise Akramoff. Mom and Dad spent their lives serving others wherever the need dictated. They did so with honor, sacrifice, humility—and with the hearts of warriors. I dedicate this book to them. I dedicate my life to fulfilling their legacy.

Preface

By
Dan Oestreich

Glenn Akramoff is invited in when a workplace is in a state of confusion and despair, when many are calling for change, but no one internally knows exactly what to do. To fulfill this role, Glenn has to be an expert in many things, but one especially: Trust.

In a private conversation, I recall him saying that when he first comes into a new organization, he often begins by speaking one-on-one with each staff member, supervisor, and manager. As part of that conversation, he intentionally avoids asking people to "trust me"; instead, he asks for the opportunity to *earn* that person's trust.

This is an essence—perhaps *the* essence—of Glenn's work. Authority alone is insufficient for real leadership. Leadership must be earned.

I've known Glenn for a long time. My own career as a consultant and facilitator focusing on trust-based leadership development began in the 1990s with the publication of two books, *Driving Fear Out of the Workplace* and *The Courageous Messenger*, co-authored with Kathleen Ryan. These books were focused on common fears about speaking up at work and how to build a workplace that could overcome those fears. While times have changed significantly, the need for leaders who understand the dynamics of psychological safety, trust, and mistrust is stronger than ever.

The pandemic, racial reckoning, income disparity, political polarization, environmental degradation, and a wholesale reset of the workplace—beginning with what has been called the Great Resignation—are deeply influencing how we think and act as leaders. It's not enough to be good at basic managerial skills. The requirement today is to understand, more deeply than ever, people and their needs.

The call to elevate the humanity of the workplace has never been stronger.

If you've been part of a challenging workplace, you know how difficult building trust can be. Someone from outside whom no one knows, who is coming in to "fix things," a consultant—with all the natural suspicions that go with that label—often faces an uphill battle against skepticism or outright dismissal.

And yet, that's Glenn's world, one in which he *builds* relationships before anything else. Only when that is underway will he engage people in the joy and hard work of changing their workplace.

Glenn is not your run-of-the-mill organization or leadership-development guru. Glenn is not just a change theorist or facilitator. He doesn't just consult or plan or hold meetings with the team (although these are part of the work). Glenn is actually there, on-site, in the moment, building those relationships while he also serves as an operational leader.

Glenn is there until the organization is ready to take their workplace back from him, confident in their own leadership and workplace community-building skills.

And then Glenn moves on to another challenge.

Glenn makes the point that he had to do much self-work in order to become the person and the leader he is today. I'm glad he chose to include some of the details of this journey here in this book—if only to remind us that he, too, is a human being, one who has forged his approach to workplaces not from an unending series of wins but from learning experiments and experiences, not all of which have been "successful."

Glenn is personable, genuine, and hard-working. These are qualities that reflect his upbringing and background as a maintenance worker and as someone who came up the hard way on his own. But don't be fooled. He's as strong as rebar mixed with cement. This metaphor may be especially apt given the purpose of rebar: The finished bridge, the foundation, and the girder are much stronger because of the rebar. But when the project is done, you don't see the rebar at all. It's *inside*.

You have picked up this book, so you must be curious about workplace improvement. The best way to get value from Glenn's teachings is to take his core questions into your own heart and soul. Don't just read this book as a recipe for a great workplace (it is, but don't stop there). Read it as the story of a journey by someone who is a kindred spirit.

Don't merely imitate Glenn's answers; rather, imitate the questions that brought him to his answers. In this way, you may very well unlock the treasure house of your own leadership capabilities. You may be able to awaken a giant within and change the world.

Best of success in your own leadership journey,

Dan Oestreich

How to Read this Book

These pages will come to you in two phases. You'll get the *Pillars and Keys of the Winning Workplace* alternated with short story-based chapters from my life that helped me learn about myself, about human beings, and about teams.

I do feel the book is laid out in a momentum-building order, but read it however you like. Read only the Pillars and Keys; read only the interchapters. Read bits of both. Make it your own. All I ask is that you make sure to read about Performance Flow on page ((#)). I'm not going to claim to be Ernest Hemingway or anything. I'm a maintenance guy at heart—I know what I know, and I know what I don't. But I do know that this chapter can and does turn people's lives around, right now (it did mine).

However you choose to read this book, please understand the importance of improving the workplace and the attention it deserves—because of the impact, negatively or positively, workplace culture has on the human beings of this planet.

We all spend a lot of time at work; I believe we owe it to ourselves to make that time positive. My experience tells me that the best way to do this is to make the workplace a team—a Human-Centered Team working together to feel like champions.

Contents

Chapter One

I owe everything to my parents. I look like my dad but act more like my mom. I am them both. Growing up, I watched them sacrifice so often. I watched them sacrifice their time, their money, and their energy in order to help. Not everyone in little Otego, New York, had everything they needed to live a thriving life; some of my friends didn't have enough money, some had troubled home lives, and others sometimes just needed that scoop of mint chip from the ice cream shop.

I saw my parents give so others could have.

Their help required much hard work on their end; it would have been a lot easier for Mom and Dad to sit at home and watch the tube than it was for them to go out in the community and make a difference. But making a difference was what my folks were all about. They left a massive impact on many people.

I have made my life about continuing their legacy of helping human beings. Sometimes, when I'm at the office on a Friday night, and the clock reads 7:42 p.m., I start to feel a little sorry for myself. "I could be watching the ballgame," I'll tell myself. "I could be drinking a cold one."

But then I think of my parents, and I get back to work.

Because impact doesn't come easy. A lot of people try to tell you that it does, but they're trying to sell you something. A lot of us human beings have talent, sure, and a lot of us have a great message to share, but it takes time and energy to hone what we want to say and then find others to share it with.

If a tree falls in the woods and no one is around to hear it, I am sure it still makes a sound—but if we human beings have something to say, some philosophy to transmit, without others to hear and absorb our message, it is meaningless.

To achieve the type of impact many of us want in this life, it really helps to have other human beings to work with. We *homo sapiens* are about the most social species on our planet. Our bodies really aren't all that well-suited to survival when compared to almost every other animal around; we don't have that much body hair (let alone fur), we can't run that fast, and we aren't even that strong. What we do have, however, is the ability to communicate. From our unique white eyes (so adept at communicating feelings with a glance) to our abilities with language, we have evolved to *work together*. Lone wolves in our society rarely have the same impact as people in pods working together. We came to greatness on our planet by banding together in groups to do what one person could not do alone. We know that it "takes a village"—this is true of survival, this is true of a thriving workplace, and it is true of ultimate impact. To get the most out of our lives, it takes a Team. This is when we are at our best, when our best can truly come out and play.

This is because, unlike, say, ants, we human beings are all pretty unique. Sure, ant society has its builders and its foragers, those who take care of the young and those who string themselves together to form bridges so others can get where they need to go. Ants are a great team; if you've ever walked through a forest, you probably know this. But what we humans can do that ants cannot is sympathize and inspire. At our best, we are not dictatorial. At our best, our jobs are not set in stone. At our best, we can forgive and let go. At our best, our impact extends beyond the confines of our little colony. At our best, one person, working with a team, can change the world.

At our best, the world *is* one big team.

Statements like that always bring me to think about Nelson Mandela. Yeah, the President of South Africa during the early 90s. You may know that Mandela, a black man who fought the racialized system of apartheid in his home country, was imprisoned for 27 years for fighting the good fight. When he finally got out in 1990, he worked with the country's existing white leadership to end apartheid. Then, after a lot of teambuilding, in the first open-race democratic election in that country, he was voted into the presidency.

Glenn Akramoff

Pretty quickly, some of his backers urged him–in subtle and not-so-subtle ways–to imprison the whites responsible for his incarceration. Mandela refused. He took flak from the right for his views, and he took flak from the left for his views. But he knew his country needed everyone, both black and white, rich and poor, on the same page in order to get where they needed to go.

It wasn't easy, but nothing truly great ever is. For his Human-Centered impact, Nelson Mandela won the Nobel Peace Prize in 1993.

Nelson Mandela is a real hero of mine, as he is for many people. As a leader, Mandela was altruistic–just like my parents, just like some people you may know–and he knew that everyone on his national team had a part to play in rebuilding their culture. Everyone was a vital team-member in the rebuilding of South Africa.

I feel that every leader–in business, in sports, within the home–can learn from leaders like Nelson Mandela. He stood up for what was right. He worked with his nuclear team to create a bigger team. He was not exclusionary; rather, he looked at the organization for which he was responsible and found the ways to achieve the most, together.

The great Pericles did this for ancient Athens. John Adams was instrumental in building bridges across the aisles in the early days of our own country. My parents did it for Otego, New York. *I* hope to continue to do it for organizations of all kinds for the rest of my days. I know I won't do it alone. I know that I *can't* do it alone. I know my message to create Human-Centered Teams will only happen through a team.

That will be my impact.

A lot of our impact, I feel, is like the wind. We cannot see the wind; we can only see it as a manifestation of what it impacts. The tree sways, the desert sands shift. It's the same for us human beings. Without a team to impact, there is no impact.

But we don't have to be Nelson Mandela or John Adams to have a big impact. Every one of us, no matter who we are, what we look like, or what we are good at, can live this type of life. We can *all* be leaders, no matter if we were the valedictorian of our high school or if we dropped out of high school—as long as we listen and are relatable; and as long as we have a stout, inclusive ethos.

You don't have to have a sword tapped on your shoulder to be a knight. Human beings follow truth. Human beings follow courage. And these are two things that we can all do and be.

The Six Pillars of
Workplace Culture

Pillar One
Culture

Many workplaces put a lot of time into their mission statement. The boss and leadership have crossed all the Ts and dotted all the Is. It's got big words and everything. They're proud of it. But none of it means anything, anything at all, if the frontline employee doesn't buy into it.

That's because culture is often a bottom-up thing and always comes from within. If a culture is dictated by the few rather than lived by the many, there is no culture—no positive culture, at least.

So, when I get invited out to a client's location, I know the best way to measure the culture is not to read the literature but to talk to the frontline employees. The first thing I do is go out into the trenches and talk with the people there. When I speak with these team members, I get a real good sense of what the organization's culture truly is. Spoiler alert: It's not always what the mission statement says it is.

After I've met with every member of the front line, then and only then do I go and speak with management to hear what they believe their workplace culture is—how they see it. Then I compare their beliefs to what I'm actually observing from the front line.

If management's beliefs and the frontline's actions are in alignment, that's a really good sign. All too often, though, they simply are not. That's when you have to get to work and start creating a more positive, meaningful culture.

True culture-building comes from the bottom up. So, I go back out and meet with each front-line person again. I bring some questions with me. One of them is simply, "What do you like about your job?"

I ask the question to everyone, and I learn a lot. Then I ask the follow-up: "What do you not like about your job?"

This answer often tells me even more, both about the individual and the wider culture as a whole. Their answers are my entry to "the change process." How can I help this team that is performing below its potential? How can I improve this workplace?

Well, it starts with the rules. When a culture is created—be it governmental, familial, or in the workplace—it comes with all sorts of rules. There are the written rules (the constitution-type things that leadership hopes will be done), and then there are the unwritten rules (what actually goes on).

In essence, it is the unwritten rules that show you if the written rules are understood, and they go a long way to determining the value of your culture. Unwritten rules can serve to strengthen the written rules, or they can serve to all-out undermine them. Therefore, no matter where a workplace culture exists on the scale of positive-to-unhealthy, a study into the nature of the unwritten rules reveals a lot.

If, say, "not pulling your weight" is breaking an unwritten rule, that tends to be a sign of positive culture. If it breaks an unwritten rule, however, to "outperform expectations"– like I've seen so many times–that is something that needs to change.

To make this change, the first thing for leadership to do is to become aware of it. Too often, leaders are blind to their team's unwritten rulebook—and to make a change in anything, we must first realize there is a problem.

After you've identified the issue, the second thing to do is try to find the origin of the unwritten rule: When, where, and by whom it was created in the first place. This can take a little bit of archeology. Once you've found what you're looking for, then go into the team and talk about it; talk about the *whys* behind the unwritten rule's inception. This is a big part of my work with cultural improvement. I'll bring an unwritten rule to light, something like, "It's okay to complain about a problem, but fixing it is out of the question." I see this one in various iterations all the time. It's human nature, and it shows up in our workplaces. It's just not very beneficial. So, we'll talk about it. We'll talk about why that type of culture exists. We'll try to change the language of it, alter the culture more toward something like: "If it's to be, it's up to me."

It helps. It helps because the words we say have power. The words we tell ourselves and others are the determining factors for a culture. The cultural glass is either half empty or half full, solely depending on what we say it is.

Another unwritten rule I often see when I'm called in to right the ship is "be nice at all costs." I know, on paper, it may read like a good rule: Show the pearly whites and don't make waves. But if "nice" is our ultimate goal, the goal above all else, then we human beings lose out on three critical things—honesty, accountability, and "the challenge." There are times when doing the right thing is not necessarily doing the nice thing. Good teams sometimes can and do get after each other. It usually shouldn't be a frequent thing, but it mustn't ever be a never thing. A good President, for instance, should not stack their Cabinet with "yes people" but with honest, integrity-rich people who will give their input even if it is opposing. Abraham Lincoln was famous for picking a "team of rivals" for his cabinet—and it helped his culture. It helped him lead. That room was not always the nicest place, but they were honest with each other. They were allowed to tell it as they saw it—and they did. They held each other accountable and challenged one another to do historically great things.

Great things often need varying viewpoints by which to be achieved. Varying viewpoints often come with debate. In the right balance, this is healthy for a workplace.

I have a friend who's a football coach, and he tells me that he doesn't feel ready for the first game of the season until there's been at least one good fight during training camp and while outside of wearing a sumo suit at an end-of-season party, I would never advocate for anything as such in a regular workplace, the essence holds true.

Challenge is a large part of what makes human beings "go." It is the same with workplaces. The unwritten rule of "being nice at all costs" is a detriment to it. So, if and when you identify it in your culture, learn from Lincoln and encourage a little debate every once in a while.

Another unwritten rule that I see dictate an organization's culture, perhaps the biggest one, is "the story we tell about ourselves." Psychology shows us how human beings truly *are* little more than the story we tell about ourselves: The person who tells themselves they're too shy becomes shier. The guy who is "only good with numbers" never picks up a guitar because the word "musician" isn't in his vocabulary. Similarly, when an employee tells negative stories about their workplace, those stories become a reality; realities like: "What I do doesn't matter that much, so who cares if I don't work hard?" realities like "I am not going to be the *only* one to work hard around here," or the all-time most detrimental, "We have *always* done it this way, so that's the way it is."

These stories a team tells about themselves give a huge "why-lens" into their culture—what they do and how they do it.

One of my favorite examples of this effect comes from my son Josh, back when he was just starting out and trying to find meaningful work. He got a temporary job working at a small government agency that, among other things, had a marina to take care of. Eventually, they trained Josh on how to read the water meters for all the boat slips. He was excited to show what he could do.

"Okay, Josh," his boss told him, "You have two days to read these water meters. So, that's sixteen hours of work."

Josh nodded eagerly and went off to read the meters. He went out and was so gung-ho that he read those water meters in a day-and-a-half, getting the job done ahead of schedule.

When he came back to talk to his boss, Josh was excited to tell of the good news. "All done and ready for something else to do!"

"Whoa, slow down, Josh," he was told, "I said you have 'sixteen hours' to read those meters—so you've got to take all sixteen hours."

Josh was taken aback by the flak he was getting. He didn't understand. What he didn't understand was that he'd just broken an unwritten rule, a story that this company had been telling about itself for a long time: "We decide how much time a job takes, and then we go out and don't do it any slower—or faster."

I find versions of this story often in my work. Many stories we tell about ourselves exist to slow things down. They exist to ensure that no Einstein's rise among the ranks. A lot of unwritten rules exist to maintain the status quo—even if that status quo is not healthy or productive.

It's human nature.

And it's echoed by our keyboards. Despite our superfast computers, our laptop's keys are laid out nearly identically to how they were on our old typewriters. The thing is, though, the keys on that typewriter were placed with a specific aim: To *slow down* the human being. The key's grid-pattern was devised to slow down the typist so the machine wouldn't get jammed up and bogged down.

But in the 2020s, your Dell Inspiron 3000 isn't going to get bogged down by someone who can type fast (we'd be able to type faster if we didn't have to use our pinky finger to strike "s" or reach lower on the board to hit the "m," etc.). Yet, 99.9 percent of us use the same intentionally bogged-down design today because it's the way that it's always been done, and when this type of thinking infiltrates the workplace–things done a certain way for the sole reason of "it's how it's always been done"–championships aren't won.

Championships are won when old things are seen anew. When you know you have the key players, but the victories just aren't coming, your culture is the first place to look. Identify your team's unwritten rules. Identify the stories your team tells about itself. It is possible to turn something from half-empty to half-full by the words we use to describe it. To rebrand or rebuild your organizational culture, look to the front-line employee and change from the bottom up.

Character

Otego was your typical super small city where everybody knew everybody. My dad was a New York State Trooper. We didn't have a local police department, so the "staties" did it. I'm sure you've seen them portrayed in mob movies and such, but my dad was one of the good ones. I've still never met anyone as honorable as a man as he was. People saw it in him. There were people who actually requested to be arrested by him because they knew he was just. Everyone knew that as long as they extended a branch of respect, they would be treated with respect by my father.

As a young boy, I observed this, saw it, and internalized his character. One of the reasons was that we always had the radio scanner going—out in the car or at home in the kitchen. We did this so my dad could follow along with what was going on, always eager to help out. I saw him do that more than once. One night when I was about 13, we were driving to dinner, and a call came through the scanner. It came from just down the street from our house. Two officers were in trouble. I heard the call come in and recognized the name: "Merv." Merv was not a guy I would want to be in trouble with—a huge guy just itching to test out his strength. I also knew that the officers on the call were relatively small guys. The call stated that when they'd tried to arrest him, Merv had taken their nightsticks from them and started to whale on them. Firearms had been drawn. It wasn't a pretty scene, and things sounded like they could go real far south real quick.

"We're still going to go to dinner," my dad announced from the driver's seat, "but I just have to make a quick stop first."

Dad arrived on the scene. Merv was still holding the two nightsticks, his fight-or-flight instincts having turned on and all gathered in the "fight" zone. My dad parked the car, and I watched him get out. He walked slowly over to Merv, speaking softly, so softly that the two cops and Merv had to literally lean in to listen (this was a technique he often used, a way to disarm the situation).

"Merv," Dad almost whispered, "let go of the nightsticks. You are going to be alright. Just let go of them, put them down."

"I'm afraid they're going to kill me."

Still, with his voice soft, my dad told the officers to put away their guns. He turned to Merv. "Okay, now tell me what happened."

Merv then gave his side of the story. Even from his telling, it was apparent he was in the wrong. But my dad has calmed the situation and *improved his workplace*; he reset the culture of the team involved, so now he could talk to Merv as a human being, heart to heart.

"Okay, son, so you didn't do the right thing," he said, "and you know it. You didn't do the right thing by stealing the nightsticks, either. But Merv, you're going to be fine. Nothing is going to happen to you. Assume the position."

My dad walked up and performed his duty, calmly putting Merv in the back of the car. He told him that he would be fine, that he was safe. He tells the officers the same thing. That "everything is okay, that everyone will feel and be safe."

A situation we've all too often seen end in bloodshed, my father was able to solve peacefully. And efficiently. And amazingly. All because he treated the other guy like a human being. He tapped into the emotion of the moment and recognized the fear of the situation, working with a Human-Centered approach to create results. He made it about those who were involved rather than himself.

When other people's blood pressure ramped up, my dad got calmer. "It's my job," he'd say, and with ice water in his veins, he would make situations better.

As leaders in organizations, I've found our job is not too dissimilar from what my dad did that night. Bad things happen. What really matters is how we respond to the situations presented to us.

Pillar Two
Structure

There would have been no Roman histories remembered today if they did not have a solid structure by which to build the great cultural things they did and achieved. It is the same with modern workplaces—on a smaller scale perhaps, but of no less importance. A good structure will keep something going for a long time. A bad structure will tear something down before its time.

It's that simple.

It's just not always very simple to see, in the moment, if your structure *is* building up or tearing down. Your structure–the act of putting the right players in the right positions for individual and team success–has most likely become so ingrained that it has become invisible. It is rare, I find, that a company regularly looks at its structure, and because of this, a company's structure can almost gain this power over the organization. It is like the bull that takes the reins; because of its power to be invisible, the structure too often gets to stick around unchecked.

I often find the *only* time that leadership comes to believe structure-change is even worth looking at is when a team-member leaves. It's like, "Well, now there's this natural power vacuum so let's finally take a look at that ol' structure."

But this is reactive thinking rather than preemptive thinking. Championship teams are not made this way. Unlike what I observe in most workplaces when I'm invited in, most organizations don't take the time to look at why they are doing certain things structurally. To be a great leader, do it early and do it often. One of the best ways I've found to look at it is to ask the question: "Is each person on my team doing what they are best at?"

Too often, they're not. A big reason for this is that I find that most companies create the position first and *then* hire the candidate to fit it. While this may appear good on paper, its application does a disservice; the human being you hire, great as they may be, will not fit into a pre-made peg as well as the human being can create its own one. Yes, there will be certain tasks in the job that must get done and certain expectations that must be met, but just because something exists outside the words on the job-description, they should not be off-limits.

We are not ants. We are at our best when we can use creativity to achieve our goals. Stringently fitting the human to the position hinders this. Therefore, I say flip the script:

Hire the human and make the position fit her. Have your structure be one that "allows the position to let the person do what they are best at." This allows for the 101 percent that, when added up throughout your team-members, makes for a championship-caliber outfit.

Everyone you will ever work with has a skillset unique to them. Even if two people went to the same high school and took all the same classes together in college, they will come out of their education differently. The same goes for people who learn on the job. We will be drawn toward different interests and therefore become better at those than others. The inverse will be true as well. We human beings are all different, possessing a completely unique skillset to the other 7,999,999,999 people on the planet.

But I still see people in workplaces in the wrong spot all the time, shoehorned into a certain position and just eking by as a round peg in a square hole. The player is playing the wrong position, and the team is losing victories because of it. This is a structural issue—and it is both hurting the human being and the bottom line. Things can and must improve.

As I write this out, my old friend Jane comes to mind. She was an administrative assistant who was good at a lot of things and had a real knack for business. She could cast a financial analysis, organize the heck out of events, and was the best proofreader I ever saw. Jane was a smart cookie. She proved to be a go-getter and became a go-to person within the organization. Her role kept expanding. Then she took on more. She was able to use her creativity and do what she was best at, and she astounded many as she transformed her role.

The fact that the organization had the structural ability to allow Jane to expand her role was remarkable, but when she was promoted, and the job she was initially hired for was looked to fill, we reverted right back to the old, tired standby: We wrote out the description, hired someone for it and then expected them to be exactly like Jane.

Not smart. Pretty dumb, actually.

We hired Frank, and we loved what we saw. We were excited to bring him aboard. But then, the first thing we did was shoehorn him into the expanded position that Jane had created for herself. We thought, hey, she was hired as an admin and came to lead the budget process, so that should be part of the fixed position, right?

Wrong.

Why? Because while Frank had his genius realms where he could rattle off fifteen tasks like he was a chef creating a signature dish, he used different ingredients than Jane. Frank was great at things that Jane wasn't, and vice versa.

In time, we were able to see our structural error and correct it (that was a good aspect of our structure, the fact that we allowed ourselves to update it and take a new look at it). So, we added some flexibility, allowing Frank to hone in on what he was good at—drafting reports, social media posts, and creating presentations. We allowed him to go and be great in his own spheres of excellence. We absorbed some of his other tasks (things that Jane had done well) to other people and let Frank celebrate who he was at work. When he was allowed to do that, he expanded his role–just like Jane did, but into different areas–saving *other* people time on *other* tasks, and a great balance was found.

It was the same balance we had with Jane, just a different weighting of the scales to get there. The workplace performance thrived because we allowed the structure to morph with the new hire. I advocate this practice in every organization that wants to excel.

To do this, to help our structure lift us up, we first must be able to admit that we may have been wrong. This is not the easiest thing for us human beings to do. But, when it is true, it is absolutely necessary.

And your structure is absolutely necessary.

The thing is, unlike culture and its bottom-up formation, the structure starts at the top and works down. It starts with management, with leadership. It pays to first see if *their* role embraces *their* skillsets because if things are off even slightly at the top, the trickle-down leads to vast chasms by the bottom.

I find all the time that CEOs try to fit themselves into preconceived roles that aren't suited for them. I'm as guilty of this structural fallacy as anyone.

When I started consulting full-time, it was just me. *I* was the company—and because of that, I had to do pretty much everything, a lot that was outside my areas of expertise. I did a lot of tasks that would have drained me if I had kept up with them. I needed to focus on what I was best at—the coaching, not the back-end stuff. Still, even as we expanded, I didn't want to give up control. It took me a long time and a few missed victories, but I finally saw the light, and we restructured how the team did things. Josh absorbed many business ends of things; Mary kept everything moving behind the scenes; Sarah took over our video creation, and Carrianne supported our social media avenues. As a result, *my* performance got better because I was allowed focus on the things that I did best.

Because of our restructuring, we started getting a lot more victories. I see it happen like this all the time in organizations across the board.

Baseball, Frontiers, and Legacy

The Otego village and city ship were small—about 3,500 people spread out around a few miles of farms, streams, and homes. There wasn't much to do, but I was a pretty good athlete, and I loved baseball. During the summer, I'd go down to the field with my buddies and my brother Bob, and we'd play all day. Sometimes there'd be fifteen or twenty of us out there, taking batting practice and playing games or just playing pepper or taking ground balls for hours. The movie, *The Sandlot*, was not too different from my childhood.

We even had a pool and our own versions of Michael "Squince" Palledorous and Wendy Peffercorn. It was the 1970s. Football wasn't what it is today, and baseball was still The National Pastime in a big way. Baseball was life; we were outside until dark with a bat and a ball. No cell phones needed. Nah, that stuff was for *Star Trek*.

On those rare off-days from the ballyard, we'd go into the wilderness, out in the woods climbing trees and looking for foxes; we'd swim in the river, build lean-tos out of deadwood and explore like we were The Lost Boys. There were many frontiers out there, a few fistfights for sure, and a lot of figuring it out on the fly. We were off with the sun and home for supper. It was good for us. Good for learning about human beings, good for learning about Team. We trusted each other with our lives out there. We all knew we could take some risks because everyone else had our back, and it made us, individually and collectively, as great as we could be.

Still, while we were out playing baseball all the time, just like in the movie, we hankered for some competition against other squads—and to play on a field not ambushing us with bad hops and skinned knees everywhere we looked. It's just that we didn't have any organized team options. After little league was over at age 12, there was nothing for us teenagers to do. Otego just wasn't big enough to support a league. So, I got out the newspaper one day and did some research (Yeah, Google may have helped here, but I made it work). I went to the sports section, flipped some pages, and read down into the fine print below the fold, and there it was—there was a team up in Oneonta! An actual organized team that traveled around and played other towns.

But they drew from a big population, and not nearly everyone who wanted to make the team did.

I would have to try out. I knew I was a good ballplayer, but it was by no means a guarantee. Even if I did make the team, I didn't know if my parents would be able to sacrifice all the driving time and gas money getting me to and from practices and games. I wanted to put on a real uniform and play a game against other kids with umpires and white baseballs, but I was stuck.

Not to worry. Dad caught wind of my research. As he would, he found a unique solution—one that helped not only me but a lot of other people as well. First, my dad found an ex-ballplayer in town who knew baseball backward and forwards. Then, he wrangled in some local businesses as sponsors, found a big lawnmower, and my father created the first-ever Pony League baseball team in Otego, New York.

It was awesome.

In a city of 1,500, we managed a stout twenty-five-person roster (my dad even drove a lot of the boys to and from practices and games). We played hard, and we played smart; we had a lot of fun playing "the old ball game." The team quickly became the center of the city's activities during the summer months. The field became a structured place for community entertainment and connection. We learned many lessons and found a lot of joy out there—all thanks to my dad and a lot of other people who helped out.

The Otego Pony League played consecutively, every summer for 39 years, a heck of a legacy for my dad. I remember going back in 2012 and watching as they hosted a big tournament. They'd named it the George Akramoff Memorial, and I flew out to New York to take it in. The kids played at a high level, and great sportsmanship was displayed. The kids had a great time.

At the end of the tournament, my brothers and I asked the community to pick an unsung "non-player hero" for the tournament—a parent or town-member who did all the little things without thought of personal reward.

They chose the manager of the Otego Team, a guy named Rick, who had sacrificed so much that summer to make the league and tournament happen. Rick was a great guy who almost didn't even want to accept the award, deflecting by saying how it was "all about the kids."

I got to talking with Rick, and you wouldn't believe it—but it turned out that he'd bought and now lived in my childhood home!

That coincidence has always amazed me. Maybe there's no such thing as coincidence at all.

Pillar Three
Systems

M y wife watches this program on TV where these people live in a house that is a mess, doing so for years on end. The premise is that they were trying to get their place fixed up but had contractor problems or something, and so the house has been left looking like a half-completed construction zone for eight years. And the family has just been living there, "dealing with it."

This little television show is an excellent example of what *most* human beings end up doing—we put up with things. Often for far too long. It amazes me; we either get used to something that is less than what it should be, or we come to think it is somehow what we deserve. So, rather than fixing the crux issue, we find workarounds to deal with it.

These workarounds become entrenched, becoming part of our systems—how we accomplish our work, but workarounds are not a positive part of a functional system. It's just that we can become possessive of them and get ego-attached to our little workarounds. So, they stick around.

I'm a great example here again. Let's take my workaround with my old cell phone. I've always disliked changing them, so I will run my phone down to the bitter end, down to where I almost have to keep the thing charging at all times if I want to use it. I live with it and deal with it, even though the system is not really working. I create workarounds like keeping the thing perpetually charging, dealing with dropped calls, and losing important texts and unsent emails. I do this because I don't want to change my routine.

But "routine" can be a dangerous word, especially with systems. Routine can keep us obedient to something that no longer deserves our obedience—like the half-fixed house someone lives in or my antiquated cell phone.

I put up with that old, semi-functional, half-broke system for a long time. Much too long. When it finally would no longer even turn on, I did an about-face and went out and bought a new one, dreading the two-and-a-half hours it would take me to transfer everything over and set the thing up.

To get beyond that malfunctioning workaround system that had become entrenched, I had to put in some work. I had to put in some money and time to get my system back up to functional. But when I actually went out and did it, I found that I had created a big boogeyman in my mind that didn't need to be there. Like a lot of systems changes, I found that setting-up my new phone was way easier than I thought it would be. It just took a little bit of initiative. In about 45 minutes, I got my system updated and optimized.

I couldn't believe I had waited so long to do so. It was truly a delight to take that first call where I wasn't tethered to a plug, where I could actually use the thing as a cellular phone and not some expensive landline. It was so easy, so simple to change. I just first had to realize that I had to change.

As happens with a lot of systems analysis, I used that change as an opportunity to go even further; had I never gotten a new phone, I would have never looked at all the apps and realized that they were mostly all either extraneous or in the wrong place. Some of them I kept, others I deleted or updated to a better version. The more I changed, the more I wanted to change it. I came to look at it as a full-on systems update and took advantage. Gone were my workarounds.

But my fault is the same as most of us—I had gotten so used to doing something a certain way that I was on autopilot, no matter that that autopilot wasn't getting me where I needed to go. I was so committed on an egoic level to that autopilot that I saw no other way.

Until I was forced to.

In workplaces, though, you often can't afford to wait that long. If we wait until our systems break down, we will lose too much time and energy in rebuilding it. So, looking at our systems and making sure they are fully functioning is a good practice to adopt. An ounce of prevention can and does equal that pound of cure.

It is fascinating to watch someone defend a system that doesn't work, defending it to the bitter end. This comes in all forms. One of them that many organizations can relate to is the "timesheet process." I mean, does anyone really enjoy it?

This system is meant to provide transparency and accountability for hourly employees. It is undoubtedly a worthy goal, but, like many things with good intentions, it can manifest in negative ways.

A past organization I worked with had "the timesheet blues," for sure. When timesheet day came (I was told when I joined the team), everyone cringed. As I observed the system they used to complete the process, I was amazed at the tedium and lack of efficiency, at the craziness of it all: The employees entered their time into a modified spreadsheet. Then each employee had to print out the timesheet so they could physically sign it. Then the sheets were reviewed and signed by the supervisor. Then they were shipped to the department's administrative assistant, who double-checked the math. Once this was done, the admin scanned them into their personal computer drive and emailed them over to the payroll team. The payroll team then printed them back out, triple-checked the math, and filed all the signed forms, entering each of them into the finance system so the whole thing could be tracked by payroll through the budgeting process. Finally, in this all-too-common roundabout way of doing things, the team sent the timesheets to the payroll company, which electronically processed the paychecks and delivered them back to payroll for dispersal.

Wow. Talk about wasted energy.

After I deduced this laborious process, I realized something needed to be done. "I am curious how this system was created to meet the need?" I asked.

"It took us years to make it work this well!" I was told, not really getting an answer to my question.

"How long does the process take, from the time the employee enters their time data to when the check is processed?"

"We have it down to fifteen hours," a proud payroll team member chimed in.

Fifteen hours? To process a time sheet and turn it into a paycheck? Systematically, I knew there had to be another way, but panic ensued when I mentioned that I might be able to find an improvement or two.

Why? Because of the human tendency to deny that change is necessary.

I went to work, and after a few long talks and some good back-and-forths, we cut the painstaking payroll process from 15 hours to 45 minutes.

A new system—a new approach, the ability to look at something with perspective and then act decisively—was all it took, and it gifted the organization 14 hours and 15 minutes to put their energy toward something else, which, after a while, everyone came to see the benefit of.

Systems go beyond cell phones and payroll into everything we do in the workplace. Systems are how we get things done. Systems are anything that helps the final product become the final product. If you have a broken system, a clever workaround is only a Band-Aid on a deep and bloody gash. It doesn't fix the problem; rather, it is a sign that you have something wrong and that something needs to be healed.

Take a look at your systems. All of them. But beware! A lot of them will have become so entrenched that they become invisible. Take the time to find the perspective to see a workaround as a workaround. Then be brave enough not to continue with it. See it as the problem it is and then fix it for good. Organizational success depends upon your systems serving you at the highest level. The key is to look at them periodically and to upgrade or replace them before the emergency light goes on.

There are no shortcuts in life. If you can find a way that is more efficient, it should simply be "the way." Take a little time up front to look at your systems—and it will yield a ton of valuable time on the back end.

Change

When I got to be a teenager, I was wild and free. I did a lot of stupid stuff. I drank too much, picked fights for fun, drove my car too fast, and even floated down the river in the dead of winter on broken ice. No risk was too great.

Plus, I was not a particularly good student. I was told, a lot, that I was not living up to my potential—so much so that I don't like the word "potential" anymore.

It's just that my goals were different from what others wanted them to be. Did some people look up to me? Yes. Did others look down on me? Yes.

When I was 14, I looked old enough to go into bars, so I did. Too often. I was unapologetic about it. I thought I was a real big deal, real mature because I could get in and throw back some beers where my peers could not.

I was a little lost. In school, I was bored in most of my classes, but there was one class that was different: My homeroom history class. For some reason, I was drawn to history—I felt like it was a psychology, sociology, and economics class all rolled into one. I didn't jive with the equations of math class or the concepts of my science classes, but I did come to feel that by learning about humanity's past, I could help our future. Plus, I respected the heck out of our teacher, Mr. Strom. One day, he brought me aside and pointed to a quote he had up on the wall:

> The reasonable man adapts himself to the world. The unreasonable man doesn't. All progress lay with the unreasonable man.

Mr. Strom looked at me from underneath his eye-glasses. "That's you, Glenn," he said thoughtfully.

"Which one?"

"The latter."

I reread the quote and absorbed my teacher's words. Right then, I knew I would not follow what everyone expected of me. I would be unreasonable. I would create progress.

As the pages keep turning, it will become apparent that it took me a while to find my calling in workplaces, but I still thank that history teacher of mine for helping me get here. In that moment in homeroom, Mr. Strom essentially stood up for me and challenged me simultaneously. It was a big day in my life—both in how I lived it and in knowing how a few words can inspire a human being.

Pillar Four
Processes

Human beings will do things the way they think works best for them. However, if our workplace has seventeen different people working with seventeen different processes–the way and order we go about doing our work–that is not good. The variance in how things get done from person to person will hinder consistency throughout the organization.

And this inconsistency will be felt by the customer.

The next time you have to call a "helpline" of some kind, you may feel like you're talking to someone reading from a script. Well, they probably are, and they are doing it because, for better or worse, that's how the organization you've called endeavors to get consistent user experiences. While I do not advocate the blind following of scripts, a good process, one that is in place, implemented, and sound, really helps ensure consistency to some sort of overall grand plan. Your processes should not be from the Wild West. They should not be from a script, either. The Goldilocks Zone in processes is difficult to attain but vital.

For without this balance and consistency, conflict can and does arise. Someone will say something like, "When I use this system for this process, I do these twenty-two steps every time."

But then someone else sees it a different way; they have combined some steps. "We'll I do your twenty-two steps in only fourteen!"

"If you're cutting my twenty-two steps down to fourteen steps, you are undoubtedly slighting some important details!"

This conflict arises because your processes are not yet good enough. If they were, there would be a set number of steps—and an apex-efficient number of steps.

This un-seamless process execution can both cause problems within the workplace culture as well as yield inconsistent customer experience. Whomever the customer is, whether internal or external, they may have a different experience each time they interact with your organization, depending on whom they speak or work with. That is why streamlining and consistency are the hallmarks of great organizations; and why processes are so crucial to the success of a winning team.

I know many process gurus who like to pull out for a couple of days and analyze every aspect of what they are doing and why. While I do support this practice (if you can find the time), I also know that too much analysis can inhibit being nimble as a team. In today's fast-paced and "instant gratification" world, the customer (and likely the boss) won't tolerate a delay of more than a few hours. That's why the successful modern team needs to build process-improvement into their day-to-day functions.

A good little illustrative anecdote to this point is what a maintenance team of mine went through with a snowstorm early one winter. The process they'd always used was to wait to organize until the storm had developed. Sure, there were reasons to do it that way, but it left them at the mercy of the conditions. The process didn't work as well as it could or should have.

When I was called in, I knew I needed to help make some changes. When the forecast became evident that a storm was about to roll in off the Pacific, we worked to take a more proactive process approach: We assigned personnel to specific areas in advance. We could still make on-the-fly adjustments as needed, but the troops, as it were, were already out on the battlefield.

It was that ounce of prevention equaling that pound of cure. It worked. But still, some of the folks who'd been there a long time were tied to the old processes. Why? Because we hadn't done enough training to counteract the many years of engrained practice. I knew we had to break a mold, but as simple as it sounds, it was difficult to change in one storm cycle.

One reason for this was that the managers had not been highly involved in the operation in the recent past. I always liked to lead from the front, so I worked on-site to lead the full shift. This change was well received by most, but still, there was a discomfort I could sense in others because they were not used to their leader being so present. Resistance was evident, but I stayed highly involved with the team for the entire storm. We had our battle plans but were not above amending and re-course setting.

Overseeing the large-scale shift down to the nitty gritty details, we improved our process and thereby improved our response rates to the snow and ice. Communication was high, and we kept the city a lot safer and more efficiently than the organization perhaps had done in the past.

When teaching processes, teaching with the same steps to everybody is essential. This is the backbone of the playbook, the plays that, if trained well, we can run in our sleep. Teaching the team to understand the purpose behind what we are doing, the reasons and whys behind the change we are making, is vital

Additionally, like a swimmer shaving all of their body hair for added speed, we want to have specific goals the task accomplishes. The swimmer may not shave their legs or arms if they don't know that it will help reduce drag in the water and can gain them a few hundredths of a second on their final time. So, in our workplaces, we must teach the hows and whats to why a particular process change will benefit the bigger picture; everything we do in an organization's processes must work to further aid the quest for the goal and fulling the mission and everyone on the team must know why we are doing it and be a part of the solution.

My experience in building teams shows me that constantly evaluating our processes—our workflow, the obstacles, the results—and keeping track of it all, documenting it, is key. It's key to onboarding employees so that they can do it consistently and feel successful.

For a stout process, create the most efficient number of steps and implement them company-wide. If you do this, you will alleviate the unnecessary conflict between people who do things at different speeds.

Still, you may be thinking, "But if everyone has the same number of steps and some do it more quickly than others, won't that give rise to more conflict?"

The short answer is yes, but the real answer is more nuanced. Having the same number of steps is a great accountability tool that can help the culture rise. If Joann is taking ten minutes to get through the approved process and Joe is taking half an hour, it gives concrete data that can be used to help the team. Perhaps Joe is miscast in his role. Perhaps this data shows that Joann is an outlier. Maybe it shows that Joe is not working as hard as he should be. Either way, getting your entire team on board with the same steps and the same processes gives a control set; it becomes easier to know what your most productive teammates can do while also providing insight that may help lift up those who perhaps can do more.

Sometimes you can think of the steps of your process as a "form." A lot of freedom can be found in form, just like how most of our favorite songs come to us in three-verses, a chorus, and a bridge. So much creativity has come out of this rather stringent form. When we have defined processes, human beings stop wasting energy on things that don't require it and tend to get to the good stuff.

Solid, streamlined processes help us human beings to just "go out and do."

Back to maintenance.

Back to the processes when the growing season is gone, and it's snow and ice everywhere. The key thing during a storm is to keep the plows out on the road. While there are a lot of things to plan for, keeping your fleet moving, and working, is critical. That's why what this organization I worked with was doing boggled me. At the end of each shift, every shift, all the snowplows would come back into the yard, off the road, so that everyone could meet and debrief, decompress, and problem-solve. Even during the COVID-19 pandemic, when we weren't allowed to put everybody in the same room, the practice continued; I felt it might be time to revisit it.

And then there's the obvious thing—by having everyone drive back over to the yard, we were taking them off the roads. During a storm, I kept trying to instill that the team meetings could wait. Constant debriefing is a great thing, but there are times when the job must continue before it is analyzed.

I had to speak up: "I want the majority of our snowplows to stay out on the road," I said. "I only want one or two to come in so we don't have a busy shop and so the service level will remain high during shift-change."

The organization agreed to try it out. We did a training event about two weeks before the next storm cycle and talked about how we would do our shift changes. Instead of everyone coming back in at the end of every shift to meet at the same time, we met with the outgoing crew *separately* from the incoming crew. It saved us valuable time during storm cycles and kept the team doing their job: Plowing snow and keeping the streets safe.

Still, to such a seemingly simple change in process, it did not come without its hiccups. Again, change is not easy. Routine is hard to break on many levels.

The first night, the snow was coming down heavily. Every second was valuable, but everyone was confused. Some people did it the new way; some people did it the old way. "Aren't we going to have a meeting?" I kept getting asked.

I was a bit dismayed but had to laugh at myself a little bit. I know that human beings rarely learn anything the first time and that *learning is practice.* So, I wrote out the new process on the board, step by step. Then I went over it with each team member. Then, when the second shift-change came around, it was much cleaner and faster; there were no crowds, and we kept people in plows out on the road.

By the third day of that massive Pacific Northwest storm, everyone knew what to do, and I could erase the process list from the board.

With a change in process, we were able to keep plowing the roads longer and perform better. You could see the difference in our final product; the city looked drivable and cared for, even after six feet of snow had fallen.

When that team's processes improved, they became a better team. We didn't go out and get any free agents or make any trades; our personnel was the same, but we had become better. This can and will happen with any team.

If the way we do things improves, we improve. It is that simple.

Expectations

When I graduated high school, I went to a small Baptist school in North Carolina. Why I chose a Baptist school I'm not sure, because I went to college pretty much just to party.

College was an interesting time in my life. While I may not have excelled in the classroom, I learned a lot. I was putting myself in new and novel situations, and my self-awareness began to grow. I realized that life is short, and I did not want to "be something just because everyone else wanted me to be it." College taught me to know what I wanted.

And school and textbooks and office hours weren't it.

The only class I did like was Religion. While it was a Baptist school, the professors explored many world religions with us. The material presented and the ensuing discussions, from all points of view by both the students and the Baptist professors alike, engaged me. It was fascinating, too, for me. I was enthralled to think how a person's belief systems, on one really tangible level, are really just a matter of where and when that person was born; it was fascinating for me to learn and think about how most all of us are saying the same things, just in slightly different ways; it was intriguing to learn about all the different spokes on the belief-system wheel that go down to the center-point Truth: Treat others like you would want to be treated.

I still think about this class when I'm out in a new organization, and I am thankful to those professors and my classmates for helping nudge me further along my journey. They had expectations of me and encouraged me to meet them.

Still, Religion was the only class I could actually get my butt out of bed for or away from the keggers to attend regularly. I knew my tuition money was being wasted. Early in the second semester, I called my younger brother. "How are things going?" I asked him.

He gave a blasé answer, but I could tell things back home were tight financially.

I called my mom a few days later. "I'm coming home," I told her. I wasn't going to let my brothers have their high school life impacted because of my college tuition. I knew I was just partying. I had a higher expectation of myself than that.

So, I came home and got to work, getting my foot in the door as a maintenance worker, continuing my journey, and really laying the foundations for what I do today.

I am not knocking college. I am just saying that we are all

different. I was always more engaged on-the-job than in-the-classroom. We've all seen those personality tests out there, the Myers-Briggs and such. Every member of your team will have their own predilections and avoidances, their own methods that work best for them.

We all learn in different ways. We all excel in different ways. Round pegs don't fit in square holes. The best teams understand this.

Pillar Five
External Forces

E xternal forces are the things that impact our operation but that we don't have control over. Though we shouldn't worry about them (because we can't change them), we *should* have a strategy for them. That's why you'll find that the most successful organizations always seem to have plans, even for the things they can't control.

External forces, unseen and un-strategized for, can lead to negative outcomes. However, external forces that are ready to be absorbed or reflected can lead to great advantages. The key is to find a way to keep your team from throwing their hands up and saying, "We can't do anything about this, so let's just let them happen."

As a leader—and by no means does that mean you have to be the CEO—we have to inspire the team to take action. External forces are not a "Well, nothing we can do here" type-thing. They are a building the ark before the rain comes type-thing.

In life, as in the workplace, it is not what happens to us but what we do about it that matters. In my work in the maintenance and government world, for example, we have no control over federal regulations, but we still have to implement a plan to meet those regulations that is efficient, effective, and cost-sensitive.

We also have no control over the political environment, but it impacts our operation every day. So, we have to take it all into account and not ignore it. I've found that even with the federal government, you can strategize for external forces. You can work to change the little rule in the law. It can and does happen.

The key to managing external forces is to plan and adapt. That's what great leaders and great teams do. Therefore, becoming aware and working through the proper channels, with foresight and sometimes even boldness, is vital to overcoming external forces. We see it all the time—the organization that is prepared, that has *anticipated and adapted*, looks a lot smarter, a lot better, on gameday.

Overcoming external forces is a skill we should all augment. Even back when Josh was working in food and beverage, he had to deal with supply chain issues and unreasonable suppliers, things outside his control. However, he strategized for them anyway, doing his best to understand what the suppliers needed and extrapolating a plan, partnering with other businesses having the same issues. Where the diminished supply chain hampered and hurt other businesses, it spurred Josh to act. He came out *better* because of it all. The partnerships he forged—essentially uniting together against a common foe—were an unanticipated outcome that was not a reality until he anticipated it and then moved to do something about it.

Sometimes we must merely survive our external forces. Other times they push us to act. Necessity, as they say, is the mother of all invention. It is the same with external forces. Trust your instincts here. Debate can be good, but hesitation can be disastrous. Time doesn't stand still for anyone. If external forces cause delay or disruption, you won't get that time back.

Again: An ounce of prevention equals a pound of cure.

To strategize for outcomes that you cannot control, it really pays to love the process. You have to want to be the best.

See the sky-burst Washington State downpour during the March baseball practice. Weather is out of anyone's control (especially up here in the Pacific Northwest), but every good high school and college team around has strategized for it; they go inside the fieldhouse or gym and take modified batting practice and fieldwork and can even run the bases. Sure, it would be better to be outside, to be in sunny Southern California or out in the ballyards of Oklahoma or the Carolinas, but we live where we live. The University of Washington Huskies baseball and softball teams have been an NCAA powerhouse, regularly outranking teams across the country that don't border the only non-tropical rain forest in the world. The Huskies know that the onslaught-rain is out of their control, but they don't let it hold them down. No, they use it to harden themselves and then beat the teams from the Sunbelt.

Like the Huskies baseball and softball teams, don't let the things that impact your organization but are out of your control hurt you. Ride the Bull market but always be prepared for the Bear. Plan for external forces to arise. Then, when they do, you will not be caught off guard.

If you owned a Redbox station, life was good for a while, but I hope you bought stock in Netflix. If you own a ski resort in the West, you'd better have a plan for the decreasing trend in the snowpack. If you are a third baseman, you better have a plan for that heckler in the fourth row. Whatever business you are in or team you are on, spend the time to think about external circumstances—those you've already experienced and any possibilities you may think you foresee, and then make a plan for them.

With the 24-hour customer expectations of today's workplace, many of us spend too much of our time reacting to the crisis of the hour rather than being proactive. But to be at our productive best and maintain our sanity, this needs to change across the board. The first step to accomplish this is by taking a few minutes each morning to plan your day so it does not plan you. Sure, we can always find a reason not to spend these vital few minutes, but by making it part of your routine, maintaining daily focus becomes attainable. With a stout plan for your day, the external forces of the panicked email from a peer or the new assignment that comes out of the blue no longer have the power to derail your day. When we string great days together, we essentially get on a winning streak that leads to great weeks and great months.

Things happen. Many of them seem like they are out of our control, but we can control how we respond to them. Spend your time planning rather than reacting—and you will see the benefits. You will.

Awakening

When I was nineteen, I took twenty days and drove across the country on my own. I meandered and saw some friends and relatives along the way. I was driving a car that was an attention-getter, and I had long hair. I got pulled over eleven times. I never got a ticket, though I even got searched in Texas.

"What if I decline?" I asked the cop.

"Then we'll take you in and get a court order and then search it anyway. And you'll stay here a few days."

"Well, search away then," I told him.

They didn't find anything, but they didn't apologize either. I vowed never to sight-judge someone or abuse my power as they did, and I was on my way.

I drove all the way from Upstate New York to Southern California, and at the Pacific Ocean, I turned right. I drove up Highway 1—Santa Barbara, Big Sur, the Lost Coast, the Oregon coast, and then up to Washington, to Tacoma.

It was a great trip that gave me a lot of great memories, and I was ready to start my adult life. When I returned home, I reconnected with a girl from my childhood. One thing led to another, and we got married. It didn't last long. After the divorce, I was three things: A father, a maintenance worker, and a competitive softball player.

This wasn't some beer league. It was a lot of good athletes playing hardball on a softball field. Everyone wanted to win. It was great. Call it what you want, but for my body and soul, it was what any yoga class or my woodworking shop is to someone else.

I played April straight through October, about a hundred and fifty games a year. In the winter, I still went to the batting cages and threw the ball around. Bats, balls, and gloves were never too far away. The game became a pursuit, and I think I became the best I could be. I was good with my glove, and I got to where I could hit the ball a long, long way. And I had a lot of fun.

It was a good time of life. I had some good friends. I enjoyed being on winning teams at work and on the field, and I loved being a dad.

Still, I have to admit that even though I got to put on cleats and be a dad didn't change the fact that I was divorced and lived in a little ant-infested apartment. It didn't change the fact that I was depressed, that when I wasn't rounding the bases or making a diving snag, I was living in this sort of perpetually bummed-out place. I hadn't been able to make the marriage work. I couldn't believe I'd failed. I held a lot of guilt inside, a lot of blame. Work wasn't great either. I felt like *everything* was out of my control. I felt like every external force was conspiring against me.

And because I thought like that, it became true.

For a few years, I couldn't sleep. I just couldn't nod off. I was working long hours during the week and playing with the kids on the weekends; I should have been tuckered out and in bed by ten, but I was up every night until two or three in the morning. My partying days were behind me, so it wasn't like I was out getting drunk every night, either. I just couldn't sleep. I'd lay on the couch and flip the channels on the TV screen. And every night, there he was—Anthony Robbins, that jawline and those incredibly white teeth appearing on the screen to talk to the insomniacs of America.

At first, I couldn't stand him. I'd see his face and keep flipping through the channels. After a couple of weeks, I started to pause for a second or two to see if I heard anything worthwhile. A few weeks more and the channel started to be changed a little slower. Then a little slower the next time. Then one night, I just put the remote down on the table and listened to what he was saying. He was talking about taking control of your life. It resonated. He was talking about achievement and making an impact. It resonated. It felt like he was talking right to me.

Still, eventually, I changed the channel. I wasn't going to be sold by anyone on late-night television. I would wake up tomorrow morning and keep doing the same things and getting the same results. But then, walking around town after work, I kept seeing his book. It was everywhere. I kept seeing that cheesy cover but couldn't get over the message I felt was contained inside. A few days later, I dished out the dough and bought *Awaken the Giant Within.*

I don't know if you've ever seen any of the editions (it's been read by over a million people), but the book is huge. I was initially a bit intimidated, but I dove in and started reading. I was instantly enthralled. It was this big technical manual type-thing that talked about concepts I'd never even fathomed. It spoke about the science of the brain, how change occurs on the *deepest* levels, and how to help spur this change. The ideas started to make sense. They began to take root, and I came to understand how I could use them: How not everything was out of my control, how I could change my view on things, and how I could help myself be my best self.

The more pages of the book I read, the more push I had to take a deeper look within—at me, my world, and my place in it. Like that religion class back in college, *Awaken the Giant Within* helped me on my journey. I knew I would use what I was learning every day for the rest of my life.

I read on and started implementing some of the techniques. Things in my day-to-day were beginning to change, and I knew I was on the right track. A lot of it was simply in realizing what, why, and how I needed to change.

When I first bought the book, I held it in my hand and felt it's weight. The thing was huge. *It's gonna take me a decade to get through this thing,* I thought. But then I told myself I would read it in six months. I would read it and do exactly what it said to do.

I did.

By about page 75, I was beginning to get my passion and energy back. By page 150, I started to be able to sleep again. As the pages kept turning, I started talking to people about some of the things I was learning and about some of the ideas I was having as a result. I started talking to people about "workplace culture" and about "the human being's place in it."

Everyone looked at me as if I had two heads. No one understood.

But I knew I was onto something. I knew I just had to find ways to talk about it in different ways. Most importantly, I had to start paying more attention to the dynamics of the teams I was on, both softball and work. I even began to get more in tune with the team of my own family, to our dynamics as a unit. I realized there were patterns in all of us, that we all did things a little different way but that we were more the same than different.

Absorbing the lessons of the book, my life became more about "the game beneath the game," the psychological and human factors that went into an outcome.

This deep dive into the study of others led to great insights into my own being. I began to realize that I, too, saw the world and my interactions within it differently. I came to realize my uniqueness; I mean, if I was seeing genius in pretty much everyone I met, I must have some of it in me too. Maybe it wouldn't look like what my teachers, family, or I thought it would look like, but it would have to be somewhere.

The more I read that book and tested its concepts in real life, the more I got to know myself. I realized I could talk to people, that I could lead. I always *thought* I could before, but I had been going about it the wrong way. I began to take action in the workplace and in my life. I finally came to know how to lead in a way authentic to who I was and how I saw the world. I embraced it. Before, I had been reluctant to lead. I'd been hiding from it.

No more.

There is a giant within all of us. There is a genius within all of us: That is something that every human being and every organization should know.

Pillar Six
Performance Measurement

L eaders must have a way to see, to know, if their team is on the right track. Again, here sports teams have it easy—it's their win-loss record. They get a real quick-glance standing against other teams in their league, one that's hard to argue with: Are we 14-3 and in first place or 3-14 and in last? Or are we 8-8 and right there somewhere in the middle?

Sports also lend themselves well to individual performance measurements. Did you bat .372 or .198? How many spikes or digs did you average per game? Greens in regulation? The number of assists, first-serve percentage, etc., and so on.

It's harder in most other workplaces to measure performance, but the best non-sport organizations find a way to measure both their team and their individuals in similar ways. At the end of the quarter, did you meet your target revenue goal? Did you grow your client list by 15 percent, or did you not? What is our retention level? Our emotional wellness average? Short-term leave-rate?

But some organizational work–like the great global game of soccer–doesn't lend itself super easily to measurements and statistics. The non-sport organization can learn from soccer here. In a Seattle Sounders match that ends in a 2-1 result or, better yet, a 1-nil result, there was a ton of action in that match that did not lead directly to a scoring goal. The goalie himself may have the easy measurement of sixteen saves and the one he did not. But for a full-back or midfielder, it has been historically difficult to grade out their performance at the end of the game.

With such a high level of activity leading to so few actual payoffs (like much organizational work), soccer has taken to measuring team-and-individual performance in more subtle ways. The best teams have devised ways to measure the "hidden statistics," things like the number of touches, time in possession, and how far the ball was advanced on a certain possession or by a single player. This allows the teams to measure the things that lead to the *likelihood* of success. Sure, that great dribble and pass downfield may not always lead to a goal–in fact, it will most often not–but, like many workplace practices, it is an action that puts the team in a better position to succeed.

Some companies are happy to make one big sale a year. That, like one goal in a soccer match, can win the game for you. It's hard, though, to measure performance because of all the work that got you that sale that doesn't necessarily show up on the box score. There were the near-sales. There were hundreds of phone calls and thousands of emails. There was all the human interaction. There were a ton of things that went either good or bad that did not directly affect the final outcome. Still, ways should be devised to measure them.

One big key is simply to find out which measurements really matter. Counting something just to count something is not necessarily productive. A team member who always turns in their reports on time, for instance, would get a 100 percent score on the metric. But that same team member may not be turning those reports in with any dynamic content in them. If their reports rarely contain anything that leads to tangible revenue or customer satisfaction, they become a moot point, and it does not really matter when or even if they were turned in at all.

Performance that "looks" great on paper because it is easily measurable may not always be great. A quarterback could go something like 26-38 for 278 yards and three touchdowns, and it would look great in the Monday morning newspaper. However, a further review of the game may reveal that the opponent was weak and that three of those incompletions should have been interceptions if the defensive backs didn't have bricks for hands. Similarly, a salesperson's statistics may be great on paper; but a further review of the advantages that the organization created for them may show that those numbers could have been better. Conversely, while another salesperson's stats may not look that great on paper, it may be shown with further digging into the actual situation that they truly got more sales than expected.

Therefore, it becomes vital for us as organizational leaders (or the leaders within the team itself) to find ways to measure success that tell us *why* we are or are not being as successful as we could be. If you have the greatest product since sliced bread and you are not selling it, why? Is it because your advertising is not good enough? Is it because you're not treating your potential customers kindly enough? Is someone else filling your niche better than you?

This "why" is ultimately so important because it gives us a heading forward. If we only count the "what," we can become more beholden to numbers than to actual results. If we only count the "what" and not the "why," something that is an actual success risks being seen as a failure.

Take Thomas Alva Edison—he had a pretty easy performance measurement when it came to inventing the light bulb: Does the thing turn on and off when I want it to?

Yet the Wizard of Menlo Park famously didn't proceed to find the way that worked but to first find the 999 ways that did not. This allowed him to home in on the absolute best way to create his product. Through this manner of measuring his performance, Edison came to see his failures as bolstering forces, things to be learned from.

It works that way in workplaces too. Today's technology and analytics can and do tell a story, but numbers only take us so far. Still, I go into companies all the time that seemingly rely solely on the numbers, and when things don't measure up, they drop the hammer—"If you don't reach your numbers, then you're not good enough, and we need to find someone else."

This line of thinking fails to consider that business is done by human beings in a complex world. Black-and-white numerical data too often neglects the grey-scale world in which we live and work.

If you worked for Abercrombie & Fitch in 1999, you could have written the logo in crayon on a white t-shirt and sold it for thirty bucks. With the atmosphere at the time, the company could do no wrong, and sales numbers for even mediocre salespeople looked great. When the perception of the company changed, however, even the best-designed t-shirts almost had to be given away. That doesn't mean that the team was not as good, simply that the external forces were making it harder for straight numerical-based performance measures to hold water.

Because of situations such as this (and a million others), I am wary of organizations with mantras (written or unwritten), anything like: "If you reach your numbers, you'll get bonuses. If you don't, you're gone."

This type of "no middle-ground leadership" makes human beings uncomfortable. Sure, profit margins must be met if a company is to continue to exist, but this type of boom-or-bust leadership tends to make your team-members feel like replaceable cogs in the machinery.

Which is not very Human-Centered.

It thus becomes vital for organizations to move beyond strict numbers-based performance metrics.

When we're talking about Culture, for instance, we need to find a way to *measure* that health. Sure, you could rate it numerically by the number of sick days taken, by what percentage of our team is involved in committees, etc., but it goes beyond that. I find the best way to measure an organization's culture is to go about it by looking at anecdotal kind of things. Engagement is a great one; it isn't a stat that shows up in the final box score, but it helps get victories.

Just after the first COVID-19 bans finally started lifting, I came in to work with an organization of about seventy people. A couple of weeks after I'd been there, we were finally able to recommence in-person meetings. I was thrilled.

"Don't be," I was told. "These things are pretty boring and never accomplish much."

"Why?"

"Because no one ever talks."

I'd already implemented some strong cultural practices and had seen them taking root. "Oh, we'll just see about that," I said.

I couldn't wait for that meeting to come. Days passed, and it came. Leadership only scheduled it for a half-hour—"Get in and say what needs to be said and get out."

But I knew my methods had been making an impact. I knew it would be different from their old meetings.

The meeting started, and leadership gave its spiel and expected the thing to just dwindle down as the minute hand moved across the clock. But then, something miraculous happened: Organic discussion sprang up; team-members started talking and piggybacking off each other's ideas. You could *feel* the engagement.

The meeting went well-beyond that allotted half-hour and eventually had to be stopped for time. That's engagement—and that was an easily observed, Human-centered performance measurement. Sure, it won't show up on the bottom line—but it actually does.

The Eight Keys to Building a Human-Centered Team

The First Key
Aligning Purpose

L et me tell you; a good maintenance worker does not get up at two in the morning in the January cold, throw on the overalls, slug down a cup of microwaved coffee and go fix a stop sign for the money. For that 52 dollars, it's just not worth it. No, they do it because they know if that stop sign stays down and morning comes and some SUV speeds into a school bus, people get hurt. That's why that maintenance worker gets out of bed at two in the morning in the dead of winter: They have a purpose—a belief that they are a part of something greater than just themselves.

Every organization on this planet has a purpose, or at least, it should—and every human being on this planet has a purpose, or should. To reach maximum potential, humans can't be floating around aimlessly like a leaf in the wind but must have trajectory. We must have a reason-oriented manner by which to travel. This is why the first key to building winning, Human-Centered Teams is *aligning purpose.*

Like a lot of the things I talk about, or some yogi on the mountaintop talks about, aligning purpose is an easy thing to say; it's easy to write the paragraph on the plaque and put it up on the wall. But it is much harder to get everyone to live that purpose.

The challenge is to ensure daily buy-in and enthusiasm for it. This becomes especially important as organizations grow; a purpose that may work for a solo-entrepreneur or a three-person team may not work so well in a twenty-person team or a 100-person team. As we grow our businesses, we *do* need to adapt for our growth, but we must *also* stay loyal to the reasons we founded it in the first place.

In my business, my purpose is clear. I am serving other human beings by using everything I have to improve workplaces. Almost every business, in some sort of fashion, serves other human beings. This sentiment needs to be in, and remain in, the larger purpose of the company. When I come into an organization, however, I all-too-often see that the purpose has gotten a bit sideways; I see human beings really struggling on a team or in a workplace because they've come to feel like they are serving "the master," serving "the boss," serving corporate or the bottom line above what their hearts tell them they should be serving. This is problematic because when human beings feel like they are serving a purpose that is not "a grander purpose," we lose engagement. When we lose our engagement, we give up, and we check out.

To avoid this, great leaders instill meaning into their purpose-alignment.

Money, even with as much import we give it, is not enough for the inspiration of a "meaningful purpose." A shiny new car, for instance, is not a purpose but an activity. *Helping* other human beings, however, is and always will be meaningful. Despite the stuff we see on the evening news, most all of us on this planet are good at our cores: We like to do good, we like to help, and we like to fight the good fight. When this is tapped into by a truly Aligned Purpose, good teams become championship teams.

In many of my teachings, the prescription for improved workplaces is for the entity to learn from the human being. While there *is* often a ton that the organization can learn from the individual about purpose, there is *also* a lot about purpose that the individual can learn from the organization. See, there aren't too many companies out there without some sort of purpose-statement written down somewhere. Yet, for us individual human beings, this is all too uncommon—most of us just don't write down our purposes and reflect on them. I'm not entirely sure why, but most of us don't.

We should. We should all define our purpose, starting probably when we are in high school and regularly updating it as we age. Sure, we sometimes talk about our purpose in the context of "a career" or "a calling," but too few of us take the time to write it out. Why do you want to be a dancer? What is the crux part of you that *has* to become a social worker or a doctor? Who *is* the person inside of you? These are questions that the individual in our society (again, unlike most businesses) doesn't do enough of. That is why I encourage every human being I work with, right when we are starting out, to answer one question:

Why am I on this planet?

It's such a simple yet profound question. However, my experience shows me that less than 10 percent of us ever actually ask it.

The good news? Whatever stage of your career you're in, if you actually spend the time to ask yourself the question, "why am I on this planet" (and genuinely think about it and write about it for a bit), you will instantly be ahead of 90 percent of the population. Do it.

Three other questions to ask yourself are:

What do I like most about my work?

What de-motivates me?

What inspires me?

Answering these questions helps to define your individual purpose in life. From this knowledge, you will be able to seek out teams that are in alignment with who you are.

Your life will be better for it.

Once you find a team that is in alignment with who you are—or if you're the organization, finding the human aligned with who you are—the way to keep it flowing is through *engagement*. Know this: If you're running a team where you have those who are engaged, those who are semi-disengaged, and those who are actively disengaged, you both have a problem, and you are not alone. I remember some research out of the *Wall Street Journal* saying something like 65 percent of the workforce is either disengaged or actively disengaged and that only about 20 percent of the workforce is ever fully engaged.

While disengagement is not an uncommon problem, it *can* be fixed. It *has* to be fixed.

It reminds me of Dave, a friend I used to work with. He was one of the guys who got hired with me in Olympia. We went through our first six months together, and after we passed our preliminary period, we were both made permanent employees.

I was beyond excited about the opportunity, and ready to dive into the work.

But I was thrown by Dave's reaction. "Okay," he said to me, "now I can skate by and cruise my thirty years to retirement."

What? I was ready to be the best I could be—and all Dave wanted to do was skate.

I went home that night and thought about it, thought about Dave and purposes. I knew the guy; I had worked with him already for six months and had become acquainted with his background and who he was. I thought to myself, well, this guy was *raised* with that sort of purpose. He was taught (consciously and subconsciously) by family and circumstance to get a good-paying job in whatever field for the purpose of "getting a good retirement," to go to work every day, pay the bills, get a couple of weeks of vacation a year and do the minimum until he turned 65.

Because the organization's larger purpose was not strong enough, Dave didn't buy into it. I don't blame him. I wasn't going to tell him not to look forward to his retirement, but I just wished it had been different. I wish Dave could have felt true engagement with his work. Both Dave and the organization would have been a lot better off if they were.

Very few people in the workforce today will work in the same role for the same company for the next thirty years. Human beings want (and deserve) to work their "dream job." Human beings want to be able to say, "I love my job; it doesn't even feel like work."

These statements can and do come true. They come true when leadership's purpose and the individual's purpose are aligned: Alignment leads to meaning, meaning leads to fulfillment, and fulfillment leads to the type of productivity from which championships are born.

Awakening II

I'd read Tony Robbin's book, put in the self-work, and started to feel like a human again. I started to get more wins, more victories in my day-to-day and in my large-scale life. After those six months with the book, I kept pushing and finally got promoted after an inside-joke inspiring thirteen consecutive interviews without getting one.

The lessons I learned from *Awaken* had sharpened some things within me while softening others. I believe I had been passed over for so long, not because of a lack of skill but because of a heaping of ego. I hadn't learned to quiet the little imp on the shoulder. I'd been bitter. I'd been reacting to life rather than working with it. I was probably a little entitled too. When I didn't get the first couple of interviews to go my way, I felt "passed over," and I let it be seen. It didn't do me any favors.

No one had been keeping me down expect for one person—myself. I finally came to realize this and finally stopped blaming the interviewer; I stopped blaming the system and finally started putting in the self-work. I learned from all those "failed" interviews—coming to see them not as failures but as Edison-like steppingstones, as building blocks. I stopped blaming others for my shortcomings; stopped being my own biggest obstacle. Like the Dallas Cowboys going 1-15 in 1989 to winning the Super Bowl in '92 and '93, I did the things I had to do to turn it around. I committed myself. I had a great talk with my parents. I came to discover my purpose as a teacher and as a coach. I sought training and learning wherever I could get it. I no longer thought I knew everything. Once I finally learned that easy truth, I came to see all that I *could* learn.

That's when the promotion came. It came when I stopped focusing on the goal and instead went all-in on the process.

Putting in the work on myself helped me change my lens away from myself and toward helping others. I changed my energy flow from inside-out to outside-in. By helping others, I would help lift myself up. That is how I would achieve the giant within.

It reminded me of something my old basketball coach told me: "Glenn, if you want to get open, go set a screen for someone else."

For those who aren't familiar with basketball, this means if you want to get yourself open for a clean shot at the basket, first go and help out someone else. You go set a screen on a teammate's defender in order to get them open, and the energy you create has a way of getting you open in return.

By setting someone else up for success, you often find success yourself.

For too long in my life, I'd never brought that lesson from the hardwood with me into my everyday life. Suddenly, though, it was clear as day, and so that's what I started doing. I began halting my ego at the door and started focusing on what I could do for my teammates and the organization. I started trying to get *them* open for success. Then, when I walked in for that thirteenth interview, I knew I had the job even before I went inside.

The investment in myself, like it has a way of doing for all of us, paid off.

I was offered my own team.

And it was a great victory.

The Second Key
Vision

No team has ever won the Super Bowl that didn't start out the year believing they would. If football isn't your thing, none of us would have ever heard the name "Oprah" without vision—without seeing what *could* become before it became.

We must all first see what we will then do.

That's why in creating a dynamic workplace, I find that it really helps to visualize it first. It helps to set a trajectory. Once we have something to aim for, we are much more likely to hit it. This always reminds me of those NASA Apollo missions back in my youth. Many times, those astronauts found that a lot of their fancy navigation tools didn't work as well as planned; there were times when they had to simply keep the moon visible out the window and fly toward it.

We can all do that.

Even in the workplace.

Especially in the workplace.

It just takes a meaningful vision, a vision that gives impact to every person on the team, a vision where everybody has a role, a vision where that role is aptly suited for each individual's skillset and energy, a vision where all those individual roles sum together in 1+1=3 fashion.

After the pandemic—and the major implementation and acceptance of mobile work—the workplace has come to be seen by some almost as a relic, as something not worth the money or hassle.

I disagree because, without it, vision isn't attained.

In looking around, I'd say that too much of our lives have gone digital. Many folks out there have hundreds of "friends" online, but when it comes time to ask for help moving their couch, they can't think of anyone to call. A high-five is better than a smiley-face emoji. Seeing inspiration in someone's eyes is better than reading an exclamation-point-infused email. Human-to-human connection helps visions become realities. Thus, we cannot lose the physical workplace. Dr. John Delony writes:

"As our digital interactions skyrocket, the data shows we're losing real human connection... Researchers, mental health professionals and public officials agree: Many Western countries are facing a social epidemic that's devastating for our well-being. Simply put: Loneliness is killing us. The stress of disconnection contributes to addiction, ADHD, anxiety, depression, heart disease, obesity and suppressed immune systems...[3,4]

Sure, computers are great, I couldn't do my job without them, but I also couldn't do my job with *only* them. I truly feel that human interaction, that sharing in the journey together, is vital for a collective vision. We should feel the ups and downs together, enjoy a good joke together, get to know how someone moves and works and is—not just if they stare into the camera on Zoom or not.

One of the great benefits of a good physical workplace is that it allows for things other than work to be talked about. This doesn't happen when you take the physical presence out of the equation; when your sole interactions are through emails and work-specific meetings and calls, we don't have space to talk about anything else. We don't get to know each other, not nearly as well as we do in the physical office. With completely mobile work, we are less connected, less bonded, and the team suffers.

Which hurts our collective vision.

It is when we are connected to the person across from us that the team goes far. Talent matters, but teamwork is more valuable. Business is not an individual sport—even my friend, the "solopreneur," will tell you that. Nothing in nature happens in a vacuum, and nothing in business happens in a vacuum. It takes a village. The closer-knit your village is, the better your vision for thriving.

The Spartans of Ancient Greece knew this and that historically strong people showed it to every foe they ever faced. If the battle of Thermopylae shows us anything, it's that Spartan vision could succeed even when heavily outnumbered—three hundred could take on a million.

Other than belief in themselves and great training, the Spartans' best tool was their formation, their phalanx. In the phalanx, the individual's shield was interconnected to the one at its right and to the one at its left. Alone, a Spartan soldier could never take on ten men, a hundred, or a thousand on his own. In the phalanx–the whole being greater (very much so) than the sum of the parts–the Spartan team did heroic things in fulfilling their vision.

Never once did a Spartan army hold a Zoom call. Their team was created by close proximity. It couldn't have been otherwise. It's the same with the truly great organizations of today. A broad and forward-thinking vision of purpose-driven production includes a physical office. It includes a physical office where people can feel the energies of those with whom they're working, a physical office that inspires people to do their best, to take risks, to learn new things, to stretch themselves, and be heroic.

Outside Joan of Arc, visions don't normally just "appear." They have to be thought out, talked about, discussed, created.

The whys need to be known; the emotional tone of the team understood. That is how a vision becomes a reality.

Visions also become a reality when we include the tangible benefits that the team and individuals will get when the vision is accomplished. Again, be it a buoy we are swimming toward or a Q4 goal down the road, human beings have a lot better chance at getting somewhere if we can see it.

In the 1970s, the John Wooden-led UCLA Bruins would not have won 88 straight games on the NCAA hardwood without the *vision* of their legendary coach. Though he could be fiery, the small-statured Wooden was also very softly spoken. He led his own way, often from a distance, and he was a genius at it. One of his visions was to have prepared his team so well during practice that when the game came around, he wouldn't need to do anything at all; if he'd done his job well during the practices, Wooden felt, he should be able to take in the game from the stands and just watch. He wouldn't have to say a single word to the players because he'd know his vision was understood and being worked toward. The team could figure it out from there.

The greatness of Wooden lay in how he got his teams to believe they were the best. Sure, he had some star players, but that program was built on vision—just like any great team you can think of, or any great Broadway show or quinceañera you've ever been to.

John Wooden's teams knew their vision inside and out on both the macro and micro scales. They knew where they were going and how to get there because their coach inspired them to see their success before it happened.

This phenomenon extends into every organization on the planet.

You can't have a team of twelve with twelve different visions of the path forward. It can't be Glenn's vision, or Haley's vision, or Atnes' vision. You can't love your vision so much that you become blind to its flaws. I've seen too often that leaders are unable to let go of *any* of it out of a fear of losing control of *all* of it.

This fear, however, is unwarranted—more often than not, if our vision is stout, the more we let go of the reigns, the faster the sled goes. It is by letting go of some responsibilities, letting go of "doing it all," that leaders usually elevate their leadership. When leaders let go of some control over their vision, it is given over to the team, where it is infused, and when people become infused, we become enthused. We feel more agency to control our future. We can see the vision, and so we start to live it, and we flat-out give more of ourselves.

Because we *want* to.

Critical Mass

I have a core belief that "right makes might." It is not the other way around—might does not make right. Ten minutes of flipping through any history book will show us that.

In my quest to fight the good fight, I have to admit that I find some great inspiration from fiction, too, from a movie called *Kingdom of Heaven*. It's about the fall of Jerusalem to the Muslims during the 2nd Crusade. It's not the best movie ever made, but I believe it achieves its aim. There's a speech in it that always gets me. It's told from a high-born guy to a low-born guy who's proved himself worthy of knighthood: "Kneel, be without fear in the face of your enemies. Be brave and upright... speak the truth always, even if it leads to your death. Safeguard the helpless. That is your oath—rise, a knight."

I get emotional at those words because it's the oath to essentially fight the good fight. There are a lot of people in the world who can't help themselves. There are a lot of people in the world looking for someone to help them out, to make a stand for them, and to inspire them with a vision bigger than themselves.

This is the crux for teams; they work better when they know that people have their back. They work better when they know their team stands for what's right.

If you work in a job where you question if this is true, know that you are not without power.

In order to change a culture, all you need to do is get 3 percent of people onboard for change. It's called "critical mass." The Founding Fathers spoke about it, and I have experienced its truth myself. You don't need to change everyone's mind right away. In fact, you won't be able to. But if you focus diligently on getting just a few people on board–spending the time to get the fire lit–your message will spread.

With an understanding of critical mass, I know I can come into any organization and change it for the better.

And you should know this too.

If you feel like you can help your team, you can. If you know in your heart that you are onto something–and you have the desire to fight the good fight–you can get 3 percent on board with you. When you do, the snowball gets rolling. Then, things get really fun, and you can create a lot of change.

As in the time of the Crusades depicted in *Kingdom of Heaven*, our world today has its despair, its fear, its feelings of helplessness. While our problems may look much different a thousand years later, human nature has remained constant. At their core, our problems are still the same: a

A few people have a lot, and many people don't have enough; power still corrupts, and true courage often seems in short supply.

Things still need to get better.

The important thing to know is that you <u>can</u> make a difference. You don't have to have been born a knight to be a leader. We can all fight our own crusade. Rosa Parks wasn't born a knight. Harvey Milk wasn't born a knight. Gandhi wasn't born a knight, and Julio Cesar Chavez wasn't born a knight. Yet all found the courage to fight the good fight. All helped groups of human beings live better lives.

This is because one's bloodline or bank account matters little when compared to the fire inside. We can all *choose* to become knights. We can all *choose* to fight the good fight.

Critical mass tells us that if 3 percent of us choose to take the oath, great things will happen.

The great cultural anthropologist Margret Meade says it like this: "Never doubt that a small group of thoughtful, committed citizens can change the world; indeed, it is the only thing that ever has."

Take the oath. Fight the good fight. I'm pretty sure we're almost at 3 percent, and I'm excited as heck to see where it all leads.

The Third Key
Define Winning

I remember being sixteen years old and watching the 1980 Men's Olympic Hockey Team pull off "The Miracle" and defeat the unbeatable Russians. You may know the story—just a bunch of our ragtag college kids fighting the Soviet pros who hadn't lost since the time of the Tsars. I watched the game with my brother in our living room back home in Otego. We were engaged for a lot of reasons—one being that the game was taking place only 130 miles away over in Lake Placid. The second was that my dad was doing security for the game. My brother and I sat on our couch and watched every pass, every check into the boards. We got down early, but our boys came back. Then Steve Eruzione scored the winning goal and leaped headlong onto the ice, his teammates jumping all over him. USA wins!

My brother and I go nuts. We're leaping around and high-fiving and hollering out. It was awesome.

The game was great, but what I remember even more vividly was the medal ceremony. As team captain, Eruzione, per Olympic tradition, was invited up as the lone recipient of the gold medal. However, Eruzione knew his team didn't play for the name on the back of the jersey but for the name on the front. So, he bucked decorum and had all the other nineteen other players climb up on stage with him. The whole team got up there, and they huddled together around the podium. They were filled with a sort of exhausted glee. The national anthem played. The team's hands were held high, pointer-fingers extended up in the "we're number one sign."

And they were:

With help from the Kurt Russel film *Miracle*, I'll sometimes play this scene on our visits to different workplaces for a certain coaching lesson. I'll pause it on the celebration, all that purpose-filled joy so truly evident among the whole team.

"You can have this feeling," I tell the human beings in the room, "if you buy into a whole that is greater than the sum of your individual parts—and *if everyone knows what winning means for us.*"

Sure, with hockey, it's easy. At the end of the game, you look up at the scoreboard to see who scored more goals. A stand-up comic only has to listen to hear if there is laughter at the end of her joke. A radio station knows its ratings. Unfortunately, for most workplaces defining "a win" isn't always that easy, but to achieve your goals, it is paramount to do so. Define your wins; what they look and feel like.

What a win is for your team should go beyond strict dollars and cents. There should be more emotion tied to it than straight numbers can give. Define your wins so that they inspire on a human level. Morale will go up, and the team will be better.

Just like it did back in the day on one of my city maintenance teams.

We got some winter in Washington for sure, with snow and ice on the ground a good portion of the time. We got big storms, and we were usually pretty good at dealing with them, but then we got hit with a gigantic storm coming down from Alaska. It battered the region for days, and we couldn't keep up. It overran us. We were able to keep a few main streets drivable, but the rest of town was shut down.

The thing is, given our definition of a win at that time, we performed as well as we could. When these big storms came, as long as we kept the main arteries open, we were happy. When that was done, the team felt like we'd done our job and would either ease off or shut it down altogether.

It never sat well with me. What about the people who lived on roads less taken? They couldn't even *get* to the main roads! I had to change our goals, had to redefine winning. It had to mean that *every street* in the city was plowed and drivable. Nothing less.

After some talks with leadership and the team, along with some changes to our procedures and structure, we made it happen. With the ambition of our new "win," we challenged each other. Redefining our win upped our ante and allowed us to give more. It allowed the team to be better.

91

Because of our redefining a win—what it looked and felt like—the number of accidents within city limits during storm periods dramatically decreased. It was amazing. You could literally tell where our work ended, and another crew's began. People from the community would call in and thank us: "Thank you, thank you," they'd say. "Our roads are better. Our roads are safer. Thank you."

When the team started hearing this and feeling just how good these "Eruzione moments" could feel, we started craving more victories. It was infectious. The better we did, the better we wanted to do.

And we got really good at winning.

Fast forward three years.

Our victories allowed us to pick up some free agents. We now had a bigger crew and could run 24-hour shifts, splitting the team into two 12-hour units. It was a good thing because right before that Christmas—the kids on break and all that commerce wanting to bustle—we were met with eighteen inches of snow in twelve hours, and it just kept coming. It locked down the area.

Yet, we knew how much this time of year helped the local and small businesses. The team knew we needed a win, for us and for the city. We got to work and didn't stop. The snow didn't stop. The days ticked by to Christmas. Everyone wanted to get to a friend's house or to the shops, or just get out of their homes to not get cabin fever. We were hearing that everything outside our town was still totally locked down. People were trying to do their last-minute Christmas shopping, but spin-outs and fender benders were happening all over the place.

Just not on our streets.

The calls came in again: "Thank you for keeping the town open," we heard. With the big mall out of city limits having to close up because of the roads, our local businesses had the best Christmas season they ever had.

That was a big win. The team felt like champions. We'd changed our pursuit, redefined our win. We went out, and we got it.

Take a look at your team, and take a look at defining the wins that will make your team feel like champions.

The Guy they Called Griffy

My dad told me when I was a teenager, "Glenn, a truth in this world is that the fact is you can learn something from everyone."

Like the teenager I was, I took the words with a grain of salt.

I grew up and started working. Early on in my career, I was in an outfit that had a guy on it whom everyone called "Griffy." I'm still not sure why they called him that; I don't think it was his real name. Anyway, Griffy was a jovial, good-natured guy, but everyone on the team was always sort of laughing behind his back, snickering at him, and prodding him.

I didn't really understand it, but then I observed that a lot of the derision came from the fact that Griffy couldn't read— he was illiterate.

Still, though he could not read, Griffy brought a newspaper to work with him every day. I wasn't sure what to make of this either. Maybe he was just looking at the pictures? Maybe he was trying to teach himself to read?

The fact that Griffy couldn't read shouldn't have affected my view of him, but it did. Though I liked the guy and didn't like how everyone was laughing behind his back, I wasn't strong enough in my leadership skills to do much about it. I just sort of let it all play out so as not to make waves.

Fast forward a few months: I'd just got my truck license, and they were letting me drive a dump truck for the first time. I was amped. It was going to be a challenge, and I was looking forward to a full day of learning on the job. But halfway through the day, my brakes started to hiss and whine. Then they got worse. "Damn it," I said, and I turned around to stop back in at the job site and tell my boss what was going on.

"Yeah, Glenn, you have an air leak," he told me, "Griffy will meet you back at the shop, and he'll fix it for you."

"Griffy?" I asked, not wanting to trust my truck to the guy who couldn't read.

The boss just looked at me. "Yes," he said, almost a glare in his eye. "Griffy."

So, I shut my mouth and took the truck around to meet Griffy at the shop.

Griffy was there holding a wrench. "Back it in right over there," he told me with a point of his arm.

I did, and then I hopped out, skeptical that this illiterate guy was going to have the expertise to fix my breaks. I rolled my eyes and heaved a sigh, looking at my watch. I was upset that I'd been told to work with this guy.

But then something amazing happened. I started to watch Griffy work. His hands, his intuition. I watched him read my truck like other people read words on a page. This guy, who was constantly laughed at behind his back and called all sorts of names because he couldn't read, was working my brakes like he was playing the piano. Watching him go, I knew I was in the presence of a genius.

Then, Griffy finished his work and looked up at me: "Your truck is safe to drive," he said, a big smile on his face, "now go enjoy yourself!"

I thanked him and hopped back up into the truck and finished my day. The whole time I was thinking how the guy who couldn't read did something in a half-hour that would have taken me four-plus hours to do.

It was that day that I finally understood the truth in my father's words. Griffy taught me that everyone has their magic—and that we can, indeed, learn something from everyone we come across in this life. Someone on your team may not be good at one thing—they may not even be able to read—but they have some unique genius somewhere inside them. We all do.

The Fourth Key
Defining the Season

After we define what our wins look like, it makes sense to define what our season looks like. Again, if you're coaching a team sport, this is pretty easy. However, for most of the organizations and companies I work with, it just isn't. Your season won't always neatly align with the four quarters of the fiscal year, and it won't always look like everyone else's. In fact, it shouldn't look like everyone else's.

Just as you should define your wins so they are unique to your team, the definition of your season—your length and pace and cycle of work—needs to be your own. It should be something intrinsic to whom you are and geared to what type of performance you deliver. It can be hard to pinpoint exactly "what is a season, to us?" But the best organizations do. The great ones do, and if you want to take your team to a championship level, it is absolutely fundamental to define culminative points within the year to work toward. Work months that go in a straight-line lead to work-years that go in a straight-line. This leads to burnout. Humans, like the planet we live on, go in cycles. Seasons are part of who we are. After extended work-related focus and output, our minds and bodies need time to rest. No matter what profession we are in, human beings need some sort of in-season balanced out by some off-season. This "off-season" is actually a big part of defining your seasons. We need them. Our cultures have done this since before even the pyramids were built. We have always taken time off during special times of the year—for "the spring festival" after a tough winter or for the "the fall celebration" after a long summer gathering foodstuffs and stores. Even today, we still have things like *Carnival* in Brazil or Burning Man out in the Nevada deserts as extreme examples of this need for socio-cultural rejuvenation.

Your seasons and off-seasons are linked; they should work together to energize the other. In order to perform at our highest level, human beings need to know what we are ultimately working for—and when we will get time to rest afterward. This seasonal definition of work is vital to the success of every Human-Centered workplace.

I was called out to consult with a city team a few Novembers ago. In this line of work, this should have been a little downtime after the growing season and before the snows came, but it quickly became apparent that workloads had kept up, and they were already gearing up for winter preparations without any break. The team was struggling; I could tell.

"It feels like we have no down time," I heard. Team members felt that there wasn't the time to train or recoup. Their equipment needed attention, but they didn't have time to stop and address it. They were exhausted and discouraged.

I began to talk about the need for the team to define their seasons. The employees seemed to be picking up what I was putting down, but the bosses didn't seem to hear a word I was saying. "We work consistently, day in and day out," they told me.

This leadership group had a hard time understanding that their organization needed opening days and closing days.

It took some time, but I finally convinced the brass to give the team a little offseason. You could feel the relief in the team. As I saw some workloads decrease, I saw moral going up. With a few days away from the grind, I saw an upbeat motivation, return to the office—some actual enthusiasm, that all-important laughter.

The team was allowed to slow down, to celebrate what they had accomplished during the summer months, and to rejuvenate themselves for the challenges of the new season ahead. Ample time-off was given during the holidays, and when we came back in January, we didn't come back at full-throttle right away. Instead, we got our muscles and brainwaves working again, our workloads peppered with a high frequency of meetings and preemptive groundwork as we slowly ramped up to full speed. We spoke a ton about our mission and our vision and discussed again what our victories would look and feel like. Like a training-camp, we ramped up for March 15: The opening day of our season as we now defined it.

We set up a few small projects to get some action in, in a sort of preseason. When we knew we were ready for our big projects to start, we threw ourselves a little party to celebrate our beginning. We ate some good food and had some fun and talked a lot about our goals, going over our work-plan again and constantly reiterating our vision. The energy was high. I looked around and saw a group of human beings re-engaged in their profession and wanting to prove it. Gone was the doldrum of constant year-round work. Infused–around every individual and the collective team as a whole–was a sort of inspired tone. It was an amazing thing to witness.

Opening day came, and we were firing on all cylinders. The team took off like a shot from the start. Each unit took the city by storm, fixing the rutted sidewalks, planting new trees, and refurbishing all of our parks and greenbelts. Within a week, you could see the physical difference in the city. It was like a painting, something truly beautiful. After about thirty days, we started to get messages and phone calls from our customers, telling us things like: "We are the best-looking city around!" and "I never knew maintenance could make such a big impact on my daily life!"

As our pride in the season grew, so did the production. Having been given a proper off-season and then a well-managed pre-season preparation and ramp-up, the team was able to keep the momentum going through the dog days of summer and into the closing day in late October. Because we'd put in the work to redefine our season, the team accomplished a ton and felt great about it. The pride was both internal and felt by the community.

And so, we celebrated (more on that later).

Still, to get there–to get through the entire seven-month growing season–we didn't just go full-go for the entire haul. No, we further broke the whole season down into its component parts. This gave us time for mini-breaks and mini-celebrations along the way. We broke it down essentially into four-week plans so that each month looked a little different than the month before or after.

Since the growing season so closely mirrors the baseball season, we even decided to mix in a little "all-star break" that lined up perfectly with the actual Major League one. The middle of July was perfect for both organizations. We took some time off, got rested, healed our bodies. Then we ramped up to go gangbusters and let it ride through Labor Day. We played so well that leadership even threw in a sort of first-round bye (in the form of a couple of lighter days) before the playoff-run of September and October.

The first year that team ever truly defined their season was the best year they'd ever had. It was the most productive by tangible measurements and the highest customer-response invoking year anyone could remember. The team knew what and when it was working for; it had been properly rejuvenated before the season began; it was allowed to celebrate the victories along the way— and when the yellow leaves started turning red, we all truly felt like champions because, by our definition, we were.

Life or Death

The amount of time and energy we give to making a living is immense. If we spend that time in an unhealthy culture, it erodes into our homelives. Any physicist will tell you that energy absorbed in one area spills over to the next; stress from the day's work doesn't stop just because you've gotten home and taken a shower.

This is why workplace culture is so important. It is a large percentage of our lives, and a person's workplace can be a life-or-death matter. It really can.

I'm going to tell you about a couple of friends of mine. The first is a guy I worked with, played softball, and hung out with. Vince was a great golfer, one of those natural athletes who could really swing it. He was a good-hearted soul and the best teammate I have ever had. He was there for everyone, always. He was there to encourage and pick you up.

But Vince was never happy at work. He'd been a sanitation worker his whole career. Though that front-line profession plays an absolutely vital role in keeping our society going, the old stigma still lingers, and Vince wore it something awful. He felt looked down upon. He felt like he'd been pigeonholed into his role, typecast. He felt like no one thought he could do anything else. Still, Vince came to work day in and day out, coming into a workplace where he did not feel total value as a human being.

It was sad. Vince was my friend, and I wanted his time at work to be healthier for him.

My other friend was Jim. This guy was so intent on excelling. I've worked with thousands of maintenance workers now, and Jim was the best there ever was. He just knew everything, everything about everything. It was literally like he could talk to a machine, and it would listen; a guy at the top of his profession who should have loved every minute of his work. But he didn't. He was frustrated beyond belief with how things were run and why certain things were being prioritized over others.

These two friends of mine from this team were not without the personal struggles that many of us have—but their negative work-life didn't help any. The organization wasn't set up to see any of their obvious problems, let alone know how to help. Jim started drinking his pain away, "self-medicating," he'd say—which only made his problems worse, both at home and at work.

It got bad, and I confronted Jim about fixing his alcohol problem. I spoke about working through all this together, that I would literally do anything to help him. But when I spoke about not letting down the team, I couldn't reach him. I couldn't reach him because I couldn't sell him on buying into a culture that didn't exist. He kept on a downward spiral. Then one night, he and his wife got into a fight, and Jim started drinking. That same night he was also the guy covering our 24/7 emergency calls. Jim took the call and went out onto the streets. He got into an accident and was arrested for driving under the influence.

He got eventually fired and started roaming around. I don't know where Jim is today. I hope he is okay. I wish I could have created a healthier workplace for him. I knew it would have helped. I truly do.

And what of Vince? Well, Vince went through much the same thing at work. He did not have a good relationship with it, didn't feel like his voice mattered. His visions weren't the visions he was working for; he came to feel more like a cog than a human being. It wore on him something bad. One hot summer night in August, his girlfriend broke up with him.

Then Vince drank a bottle of whiskey, put a gun to his head, and pulled the trigger.

I know a healthier workplace would have helped these men. I *know* it would have.

I miss these guys. I miss Vince and Jim. I think about them all the time, and they are a big reason why I am so passionate about what I do. They are my inspiration to continue to help, to continue to do better. They are the reason I know that the difference between a healthy workplace and an unhealthy workplace is a matter of life and death.

Our workplace should *add* to our life. It should *augment* our life. It should make our lives *better*. It truly should.

I believe that every human being deserves to be afforded this basic human right.

The Fifth Key
Clarifying Roles

When you start thinking and planning out roles for your team, my experience tells me that it pays to know everyone's gifts, skills, and passions—and then adapt and clarify the *position* to maximize them.

The truth is that every person in your organization will have a little bit different skillset. We all have things we like and things we don't like, things we gravitate toward, and things we'd rather avoid. Some of us even have gifts, things that we can "just do" that we've seemingly never really had to learn. If you've ever seen the 1998 film *Good Will Hunting*, you'll remember that Matt Damon, as the title character is pretty good with numbers. At one point, he's talking to Minnie Driver as Skylar, and she asks him, "Do you have a photographic memory?"

Will's answer isn't straightforward, and it has always stayed with me. He talks about Beethoven, how Beethoven looked at a piano, and "it just made sense to him." How Beethoven could "just play."

Skylar says something like, "Are you trying to tell me you play the piano?"

Will: No, not a lick. I mean, I look at a piano, I see a bunch of keys, three pedals, and a box of wood. But Beethoven, Mozart, they saw it, they could just play. I couldn't paint you a picture, I probably can't hit the ball out of Fenway, and I can't play the piano.

Skylar: But you can do my o-chem paper in under an hour.

Will: Right. Well, I mean, when it came to stuff like that... I could always just play.

We don't have to be fictional geniuses to have things in our life-and-work where we can "just play." We all have these things. It's just that they are different for every one of us. Will Hunting would have failed if he had to play the piano or paint a picture or hit the ball out of Fenway Park, but at the things he was good at, he was phenomenal.

Writing it out now, I'm reminded of a woman who used to work at a shop I did some work for. Where Will's gift was numbers, Rebecca's gift was people. She was the most gifted people-person I've ever seen; just a natural. She could light up a room, was genuinely curious about how your day was going, and would make you feel better after talking with her. Rebecca was a natural receptionist, and that was the role she was playing for the team.

She was perfect for the job as it was laid out on paper. However, the shop had changed courses a bit and ended up not having many visitors, so Rebecca ended up taking on a lot of admin work to help ease the load on others. She started looking over the bills and helping with new hires, even going so far as to support the managers with their paperwork when she could.

In short, her actual day-to-day turned out to be much different than what she was hired to do. Rebecca became a receptionist who ended up dealing very little with human affairs. But her natural people-person gift wanted and needed to shine. Even though she was taking on a lot and going outside of her comfort zones, perhaps to do it, some of the other employees began to complain about her being too chatty, about her talking their ears off on matters not necessarily related to the task at hand.

"She's way too into small talk," I kept hearing.

People were getting frustrated, sometimes making excuses to avoid her because they were afraid of being caught in conversation.

On the flip side, this woman who was hired "to talk to people" was getting frustrated that she wasn't getting to do much of that! She was stuck doing someone else's job. She felt her teammates being short with her and came to feel like no one respected or cared about her.

The lack of clarity in Rebecca's role–the receptionist not being able to be one (Beethoven being asked not to play the piano)–wasn't helping the workplace, and it wasn't helping her life. Her work wasn't fulfilling because it wasn't utilizing her natural and amazing gift.

I saw all this going on and got curious about trying to clarify her role. I spoke with the other members of the team: "Hey, I hear what you guys are saying, but she really is a genius people person. That's rare, special. She's just in the wrong role."

I argued that she would be better served–both professionally and personally–by transferring to City Hall to be the full-time receptionist.

We broached the idea with Rebecca, and she was open to it. We tried it out for a week to see if she felt like she could gel in a new role. She did. After only a week, there was no chance of her going anywhere else. She was the spark that the City Hall team needed. It needed the heart-centered empath working at the front desk. It needed someone with Rebecca's natural gifts.

Over at City Hall, her teammates started making excuses just to come over to the front desk and say hello and get lifted up by her conversation. People loved her interactions, loved the intimacy and empathy they felt when talking with her. People loved how Rebecca made them better at their jobs by doing hers.

When she was put in a role that allowed her natural skills, passions, and gifts to shine, Rebecca's star shined bright. Once we finally placed her in a position that suited who she was, Rebecca got excited about coming to work and got even better.

110

We moved her out of the amorphous "catch-all" she'd become at the shop and clarified her role as the human-to-human glue that held City Hall together.

She was just what that team needed. It was already filled with super smart humans whom all had their areas of genius, and when they received the player via trade, the team soared.

In your workplace, look to the individuals on your team. Look to their gifts, skills, and passions. Then put them in places where they can be celebrated.

Magic in the Cal Ripken League

My buddy Ryan had been harping on me to coach a local youth baseball team for years. But Josh hadn't wanted to play organized ball as a 9-, 10-, or 11-year-old, so I had a good excuse not to take on the time commitment. When he turned 12, and the occasional games of catch weren't enough anymore, Josh wanted to play, and my excuse was up. Ryan and I spoke again, and he gave me the final sell I wanted to hear. "I'll do it," I said, "I'll coach the team."

Josh and I were immediately excited.

In the sixteen-team, two-division Cal Ripken League, we were the Diamondbacks. Tryouts were to be held for a league-wide draft. Every player who wanted to play came out one Saturday morning to showcase their skills—swinging a bat, fielding some ground balls and fly balls, and, most importantly, throwing.

With Josh having never played in a league before, we knew us Diamondbacks would be in the lower division and would not be drafting near the top of the list. Knowing I probably wouldn't get the opportunity to draft any future major leaguers, I decided to home in on two things: Attitude and unseen talent. I grabbed my clipboard, and off we went.

It was raining, and so we were in the elementary school gym. Some kids wore baseball pants and jerseys, others sweatpants and t-shirts. Most of the kids ranged from 10 to 14, with a few 9- and 15-year-olds in there as well. I sat up in the stand all alone as I was new to this part of the community. It came time for the kids to throw—the length of the gym. Some kids had strong arms, others noticeably less so. Josh was somewhere in the middle.

Then this 15-year-old came out, a full head-and-shoulders bigger than anyone else. But it wasn't just that he was bigger or older. We'd seen from his fielding and batting that the kid could really play. So, he grabbed his ball, took aim, and threw his first throw, which hit the glove on a rope with a loud "Bam!" Then the second, "Bam!" The third... The kid had a cannon and knew the intricacies of throwing a baseball.

A coach sitting next to me leaned over and whispered, "This kid's gonna play pro ball." He did.

But I knew he would do well off the board before the Diamondbacks' spot in the draft came up. Then the next kid's name was called—a shaggy-haired, skinny 12-year-old. It was a tough act to follow, going after the future Mickey Mantle 15-year-old that had just wowed everyone.

The shaggy-haired kid took the ball in his hand, and it was like he'd never held a baseball before. He prepared to throw the ball, a right-hander with his right foot forward. He reached his arm awkwardly back, bent at the elbow, and short-armed a toss that flayed softly and hit the wall right next to him. It was obvious that no one had ever taught this kid how to throw a baseball before. Some of the kids laughed and snickered.

The coach again leaned in toward me. "This kid's gonna be the last kid drafted."

On seen-talent, I couldn't argue with the guy. His skills were the lowest of anyone out there. But then I saw something. The kid didn't run and hide in the back of the line. No, he strode back over to the bucket and grabbed another ball. He took his position and took a breath, and tuned out the peanut gallery. He had the courage to make his next two throws.

"I'm going to draft that kid," I told myself. "Showing guts shows a good attitude." Since he'd obviously never been taught to properly throw a baseball, I wagered there was some unseen talent to be tapped. He looked humble and hungry and like he wanted to learn the game of baseball.

The tryout ended, and all of us coaches gathered together at a restaurant to draft our teams. The kid with the cannon went to the Dodgers with the first pick. The first round ended, and the next few rounds played out. I was drafting a good team, and we got to the second-to-last round. I knew I could get away with waiting until the final round to get my guy, but I also didn't want to take any chances. I wanted his courage on my team. "I'll take Billy Myers," I said.

A sort of confused silence fell upon the room. "You sure?"

"I am."

The first practice came around, and I could tell we had a scrappy team. Josh was playing first base and swinging the bat pretty well. We had a kid who could play shortstop and a few guys who could throw strikes. I worked hard with Billy on his throwing, working the fundamentals of the throwing motion to ingrain some muscle memory. We worked on keeping his left shoulder closed, on reaching his right hand down and away from his body, on leading forward with the elbow, and following through to the target with the wrist and fingers. Before long, Billy was making great throws from left field in our games. He also got to be pretty smooth with his glove and became a solid fielder. It was great to see how far he'd come since the tryout.

But, as a hitter, though he'd made some good contact at the plate, a few games into the season and Billy still hadn't gotten his first hit at the plate.

Hitting a baseball has been called the "hardest thing in sports." You're given a rounded bat and a round ball and told to hit it "square." It's just not that easy; great players being lucky to succeed in one in four tries. But Billy put in the work in the batting cage, and by the midway point in the season, I could tell he was starting to get the hang of it.

I got a call the night before our next game. It was Billy's mother. "Billy doesn't know this," she said, "but his brother is about to arrive home from Iraq. He's planning on being at the game tomorrow, but he doesn't want Billy to know. He doesn't want to make him nervous or anything."

I was ecstatic. It was Billy's turn in the rotation to play the entire game, and his brother—who had been deployed for some time and whom Billy had been worried about—was going to surprise him with being home safe and sound. I had a good feeling about things as I went to bed that night.

Morning came. I got through some work, and Josh and I went out to the ballyard. It was tough not to tell Josh about Billy's brother, but I knew I had to keep the surprise intact. As the team started warming up, I saw a young man in full military-dress behind the grandstand. I made sure the kids weren't watching and walked over and introduced myself. I thanked Billy's brother for his service, and we talked about what a big moment it would be for Billy.

His brother said, "I'm going to stay tucked behind the other families and then surprise him after the game."

"Sounds good. We'll keep it quiet."

The game started. The first few innings were a pitcher's duel, and Billy made some good plays out in the left field. Then it was his turn up to bat. From my spot in the third base coach's box, I saw Billy stride to the plate and take his stance. He looked good, confident. The first pitch was a ball. The second pitch came, and Billy took a good rip at it and fouled it back. "Here we go, Billy!" come the cheers from the grandstand. Billy dug in, and the pitcher threw a fastball coming in on the outside corner. Billy fired his hips and connected bat to ball and sent a line-drive screaming out to center field for a base hit! The crowd went wild. "Way to go, Billy!"

Billy stood proudly on first base after his first hit in organized baseball. His smile lit up the grey Pacific Northwest sky. He was so happy, so proud—and he didn't even know his brother was home from combat and up in the stands.

A couple of batters later, our third baseman smacked a single, and I waved Billy around third and sent him home. Billy runs fast and slides in safe at the plate for the go-ahead run! I look up into the stands and see tears of joy—not just on Billy's family's faces, but everyone's.

We went on to win the game. After the last out was recorded, I got the ball and snuck it up to the stands with some instructions on a little plan. Then the team gathered in the dugout and selected our Most Valuable Player, something we did every game. The choice was obvious. "And the MVP is... Billy!"

The team went nuts, and we gave Billy his MVP t-shirt. He was one big smile. "But where's my 'game ball?'" he asks.

"Your game ball is coming," I told him, hardly able to contain my grin.

Then, like something from *Field of Dreams,* out from the grandstands came Billy's brother. Billy looked up and saw him. He couldn't believe it. They ran to each other and wrapped their arms around each other. Billy's brother presented him with the game ball. The whole stadium was in tears.

It was about as magic of a human-moment as I've ever experienced.

The Diamondbacks went 16-1 that year and won our Cal Ripken League division championship. Josh contributed a lot, and it was just a great season. But our biggest moment, by far, was Billy's game. Everyone at the field felt lucky to have been a part of it. Kids and adults alike. It was one of those special, special victories in the game of life.

I think back to that moment often. When I do, I thank Billy for letting me be a part of it. I thank Billy for picking up another ball at that tryout and having the courage to throw it. If he hadn't shown that courage, I wouldn't have drafted him. And mine and Josh's lives would be missing one of our best moments.

Attitude and unseen talent—look for it when you create your teams; magical things can happen.

The Sixth Key
Debrief Constantly

E verything big that has ever been built has been done so through small steps. The pyramids of Egypt were built one block at a time—putting that one block in place, fitting it to the one next to it, making it strong enough to be built upon, then growing the structure from there.

It's the same with teams. Championships are built one step at a time, and a big step in this incremental process toward getting your Human-Centered Team where it needs to be is to debrief constantly. This means that after you have set up your plan and done your work, it is paramount to then go over what you have learned. Going over what you have learned, reiterating the hows and whys, is not some afterthought to the process but a *key part* of the process.

Debriefing constantly cements the learning. Like that monolith in the pyramid, it makes it so it can be built upon to make something big.

This process should come in both written and verbal forms. When used in conjunction, speaking something aloud and writing it down (best with pen on paper) is the best way to learn something long-term. At least, that's what I find.

One summer, I was hired to help a small parks-maintenance team that had been together for about fifteen years. They'd done some good things and had attracted some positive attention, but in their success, they were experiencing some growing pains. In essence, the organization was a teenager; you could see they were developing, but you could also see that they didn't always know where they were going (or how they were going, or why they were going). The team was losing a lot of forward momentum because of a lot of zigzagging action. Details were lost in the cracks. Things were said in the meetings but not put into practice out in the field, and it was hurting performance.

To help change this aspect of their culture on a fundamental level, I began enrolling team-members and leadership in the concept of debriefing constantly. It was late August. One of our irrigation systems was down, and it hadn't rained in 84 days. Some of our ballfields looked more like hard-caked, dried-out lakebeds than lush grass. They'd become fairly unsafe; a 12-year-old left fielder was almost at risk of a concussion if he dove for a flyball down the line.

We formed a plan to fix the problem. A guy named Eddie took the lead and got to work. But things turned out to be worse than we'd even thought. The irrigation system was really broken, and standby quick-fixes weren't working.

After a few days, I went out to the site to check-in with Eddie and to see how things were going. I parked my truck and walked over to him. "How's it goin', Eddie?"

"Okay."

"And the process? What have you learned?"

"Well, first, I figured out how to open and get into the vault."

"Great."

"And then I figured out where the leak is. And so, I now know what we need to fix. I know what parts I need."

"Great. Did you write that down?"

"Yep, I did," he said, pulling a notepad from his back pocket. "It's right here."

"Great. From your notes, was there anything that didn't go so well?"

"Well," he said, flipping pages on his notepad and telling me gritty details about the next steps for checking the pumping mechanism.

"Good. And from our pre-planning sessions, what are the next-steps on that?"

"In this case, I'm going to pump out the vault so I can get into her and see what is really going on."

"Sounds like a good plan. What are your processes going to be?"

Eddie slung them to me like a teacher does a lesson plan. "Bravo. And what does a 'win' look like for you on this job?"

"Get the fields safe for the kids."

I wasn't out there to micromanage Eddie but to ensure that he knew how to fish. This debriefing was part of the plan we'd made, and I could tell Eddie had put in the time and had an avenue forward. He was learning on the fly and making the necessary adaptions when needed. He had a solid purpose and knew why he was doing the job. He could teach me how to do it, and so I knew he could do it. Eddie too. We said goodbye.

Eddie implemented the next stages of his plan, and we got word that the field was improving.

In a few days, I went back out to the site again to debrief. "Okay, Eddie. So, what went well?"

"The pumps are working. We're getting flow, and the ballfield is actually getting irrigated pretty evenly."

We walked the outfield, and it was apparent that progress was being made. "Great work. What still needs to go better in order for you to get the win?"

Eddie reached into that back pocket of his and pulled out the notepad. He read off a checklist worthy of a battle plan, how he was going to educate himself on the pipes. "I'm going to the supply store this afternoon to get started."

"Awesome. Good plan."

I came back in a few days, and the ballfield looked like a field in spring. Eddie had formed a plan, and our debriefing solidified it. In doing so, he'd taught himself how to fish. And with his new knowledge, we now had a plan for if and when the irrigation systems ever broke down again. We had a plan to keep our left fielders safe.

Whether it is fixing an irrigation issue or making sure people aren't talking behind others' backs, whether it is knowing the Q2 goals or the unwritten rules or how to anticipate and overcome external forces, continually talking out a plan has a way of hardening its resolve. Debriefing constantly calls into response the "power of repetition." When something is only said once, perhaps never even written down, the message remains in our brain, but our ability to retrieve it weakens. Our brains work through synaptic pathways—the more times we access something, the more readily available the information is to us. If something is said only once but not returned to, the synaptic pathway to access it becomes thinner and thinner until it breaks. In this case, the one-time knowledge we had now sits on an isolated island that can't be gotten to. But when things are constantly discussed audibly and then written down—reinforced—that pathway becomes like a big boulevard, and we can readily access that learning. This is why debriefing constantly works.

While the practice can sometimes be a difficult sell to your team, once it is implemented, the results have a way of coming in. In a way, this debriefing is a little like the wind; we don't see the wind, only what the wind affects—the trees it sways or the desert sands it moves into mountains. That is the power of debriefing constantly. It is a force that exerts its force onto other, more tangible outcomes. When implemented into a workplace, things get more efficient, and performance increases. Mantras and slogans become ethos'. Tasks become avocations. Teams get better. Dangerous hard-caked dirt fields become lush green havens once again.

The last time I came out to check on Eddie and that ballfield project, I didn't even have to ask any questions. He had learned the process, knew what his win looked like, and told me a detailed process of what he would do to finish the job.

"Sounds like you're on the right track," I said to Eddie, and I looked around at all the green grass on a now-beautiful field. I wanted to put a glove on and take some fly balls out in the outfield. I was happy for the kids who'd get to play on it.

It was funny, too. After my contract was up, I was invited back out to the organization a few months later—and everyone was asking me *my* questions.

I was getting debriefed. And it was constant. I loved it.

Horses

For much of my adult life, I have owned thoroughbred racehorses. It has been both a fun side project and a deep and profound education in Team.

The first thing that horse racing ownership teaches you, I've learned, is patience. That's because horses, like humans, are not machines. They are living, breathing animals with their personalities, moods, aches, pains, predilections, and avoidances.

A racing horse only races when it can—and when it wants to. As an owner, that is something you have to learn. When they are ready to run, you run them. When they are not, you don't. At first, this concept was difficult for me to get behind. I was dependent on something not 100 percent in my control (same with all teams), but in this case, I was working with someone who was not my species. We had to learn how to communicate, the horses and me. To do this, a lot of the language that I had to learn was *patience*. This was hard for me–hard for a lot of us–in this immediate-type world we live in. I had to slow down and take a step back, do the best I could to put us in an opportunity to succeed, and then see how it all played out. Working with horses has taught me a lot about the Pillars and Keys in this little book I'm writing out. In short, working with horses has helped me a lot with working with human beings because I don't think we are all that dissimilar.

Just like with any human team, my work in horseracing has taught me the importance of "having a plan but remaining flexible." You have to nurture the horse just like you have to nurture the team. Both have to train well; they can't get too sick, can't pull a hamstring, or get frayed between the ears.

In horse racing and team-building, the goal is the same: Get your organization to the starting line in as honed and tip-top shape as possible, build up as much advantage-by-alignment as possible, and then let the horse run, let your team do its thing.

Whether working with human beings or horses, this requires trust. Over at the stables, we even have a t-shirt that says, "Trust your Trainer," referring to the horse trainer—the guy or girl whose genius it is to understand the animal (like the quiet guy who lived in the woods from *Seabiscuit*). Sure, as with any entity, you must verify and cross-reference and pay attention (we've all heard about the bad apples in big-time horse racing), but if you partner with someone who is purpose-aligned with you, the trust can, should, and will come.

Yes, my purpose in owning and racing horses was born from my competitive spirit, a pursuit of elite sport in the years after my body could no longer do it. I do want to win. But for Left Coast Thoroughbreds, it's always been about the horse first. That's part of the trust. The horse has to trust us, has to trust *me*, and has to know that I will not force it to run if it can't or is not ready to.

A thoroughbred racehorse wants to run. That is what they are born to do. It is their genius to run. And so, it is my job to allow their genius to reach its maximum. The trust in the relationship is that the horse knows I have its best intentions in my heart. I care for the horse because I know the horse cares about me—like after my mom died and I went down to the barn for some solace. Mixo, a usually kind of surly fellow, came up to me and nuzzled me. He knew I needed a lift and could sense that I needed some empathy.

That nuzzle wasn't directly related to our working relationship; it wasn't directly related to our end goals—but it helped us get there. That nuzzle, like a high five or genuine vulnerability or laughter at work, showed our trust in each other, showed that we had each other's back.

This trust has led to first-place finishes and championships, to great times, and feelings of immense joy. This trust has led our team of horse-and-human to achieve big things.

"Do they know if they win?" people ask me all the time,

"Oh, yeah," I tell them. "The horse knows if they won. You can see it in their eyes."

Just like you can with your Human-Centered Team in the workplace when they win. The look in their eyes, and yours, will tell you if you've just won your championship. I hope you get to see it often because it is a great thing.

The Seventh Key
Understanding Flow Performance: Part I

O ne thing I have noticed about human beings is that we don't go in straight lines. Circles and cycles are innate to our lives and productivity. There's a quote out there by the 19th Century German philosopher Frederick Nietzsche that goes something like, "Everything straight lies. Life is crooked; time, itself, a circle."

I don't know too much about German philosophy, but I do know that I think that quote is pretty spot on. It aligns with what I've witnessed in workplaces and workflow throughout my career.

My observations about human beings and how we perform began a long time ago, back when my son was 9 or 10 years old and having trouble at school. No matter what he tried, Josh couldn't seem to sustain the workload over the entire semester. He was up, and then he was down, and then he was up again. He struggled with the grind that the curriculum was putting him through.

However, for brief periods he would show improvement, getting his homework and studying done. During one of these such times, I looked at my wife and said, "You know, he's doing better."

She took a sip of her coffee. "He can do anything for six weeks."

Initially, I have to say, my wife's answer seemed a bit curt. However, at the same time, it seemed to accurately describe Josh's performance. There *did* seem to be a pattern: After a low point of missed assignments and mediocre test scores, Josh would start getting after it again. He would show tangible improvement. This ramping up would last a few weeks, and then he would plateau at a high level.

It was great, great to see him so active, his mind and body so alert, so raring to go.

But it just never lasted.

After Josh's acceleration and productivity plateau, his study habits would seemingly go out the window and come to a crashing halt; his performance with his schoolwork would drop. Then drop a little more. And then he'd hit some bottom and stay there for a couple of days before starting to get after it again.

I observed my son and his patterns of focus and output on his schoolwork. I thought, "Wow, that's interesting. I wonder if that's just my son"—then thinking to myself, to my wife, our natures of work—"or if that's everybody?"

I studied my own patterns first. I started paying really close attention and noted certain things about my workdays (because I was me, I even charted them out on graph paper). My results were intriguing: Some days, I could do 27 emails in a row and just rattle them off while almost having fun. At other times, I charted that I could barely focus enough to write one single good email. It wasn't necessarily the content of the emails either; it was just that they were there.

My performance charts on other tasks within my workdays and weeks followed a similar pattern—at certain times, I could fly through everything I needed to get done, but two weeks later, I couldn't even keep up with the basic issues of the day.

Sitting down to tabulate my results one night, I came to realize that I displayed the same graph as Josh did. After coming back from a vacation or some downtime, I would get back to work and hit the ground running; I had this two-week period where I ramped up the pace and got better and better every single day. I felt like the Denver Broncos going to play a road game at sea level—traveling down from a mile high, they have more oxygen in their blood than anyone in the league; when I was in that ramp-up, I felt like I could take on more and more, like I would never get tired.

Then I would reach this beautiful plateau, a place of go-go-go where I performed at my highest level. My mind would be firing on all cylinders, and my work would be great. I felt awesome. I would stay there, remain there, maintain there. I would accomplish a lot during this Performance Plateau, doing memos, PowerPoints, schedules, projects, and emails like there were three of me. Things were a breeze. I accomplished incredible volumes of work in short periods of time while still keeping a constant connection to my team.

While on my plateau, I could see far. Interruptions wouldn't even slow me down. I could have casual chats with anyone for thirty minutes and jump right back into whatever I was down without missing a beat. Mistakes seemed to disappear; if I did make one, I could catch it early and fix it easily. When up upon my Performance Plateau, I also tended to be more flexible and in a good mood almost every day.

During these couple of weeks, I was truly excelling. However, I was excelling because I was maxing out my energy stores and doing a lot of reps with a lot of weight for a long time will tire anyone out.

After my explosion of production in my performance ramp-up and plateau, I observed that I stopped firing on all cylinders, and those emails got harder. I would then have a downturn of about a week where I could feel my energy waning and my performance-level decreasing.

Then I would have a day or two where I didn't want to do much of anything.

After some rest, I would begin to ramp up again.

Well, this little theory of work patterns fits for me, and it fits for my son, I said to myself. *I should look at my team.*

I was in a managerial role at the time and had a team of six. Before then, I had only observed our productivity and styles in a general way. However, with my data on Josh and myself, I started paying much more in-depth attention to how the team worked, documenting our production patterns, moods, and efficiencies over time. I even found a way to have my team record it for study—I'd have them rate their day. I'd give them a piece of paper, and they'd score their workday (productivity and mood) on a scale of one to five.

The team did this rating system for about three months. I watched the data come in, and at the end, I tabulated it all up. The results were right in line with what I'd observed about Josh and myself. My team worked, like Nietzsche told us, in cycles.

And again, I noticed the cycle going in roughly six-week increments.

But what I also knew was that leadership (and the employee team themselves) were striving for some "level consistently"— the same pace day in, day out, every week for months on end.

"The way we are working," I said aloud, "seems to be at odds with the way we are expected to work. This isn't right."

Understanding Flow Performance: Part II

I have nothing against the student that shows up every day of high school to get their "perfect attendance" plaque, but it isn't always about just showing up and doing the same thing every day. While "consistency" has always been a big buzzword in the workplace, we human beings aren't designed to be all that consistent but rather to work in spurts—and not without peaks and valleys.

I continued to observe my team. I kept track of where we were and how we performed on a given day, week, and in few-week intervals. I got inquisitive about the psychology of work, of how we human beings do it. As I watched for those three months, what I saw was not consistency but "consistent inconsistency."

I looked at my charts and game-planned. When I added it all up, I knew what we needed to do. I needed to change the expectations that had been engrained in my team their entire career. I needed to change my expectations, too, toward the team members' performances. I needed to be more understanding of the ups and downs. My team needed to feel okay about "having a bad day," whatever that meant for them.

These bad days weren't always about effort either. Some days, the effort was there, but the performance just wasn't. It was like the teammate was playing behind the eight-ball or something.

On other days, they did not even have to really work all that hard, but the performance just came. Like they were "in the zone" or something.

This was truly the first time in my life that I understood that effort and performance weren't necessarily as linked up as I thought.

Good old John Wooden had a saying about this, one he repeated so often it became a mantra for his UCLA basketball teams: "Never mistake activity for achievement." I don't think I fully understood the words until I charted my team's activity levels vs. their performance levels. Looking busy did not always mean that the job was getting done. Activity did not always lead to achievement. Sometimes, achievement could be attained without the bustle.

My data was a revelation—a revelation that I had to change the way I led.

I called a team meeting and talked about some changes I wanted to make. We began by adding another team and moving forward with our performance charting. What I noticed was that one team was still really striving to be ultra-consistent. Despite what we'd recently become aware of, the conditioning to accomplish the same amount of work every single day had become so ingrained that it was hard to break.

But "the same every time" is how machines work. Human beings aren't machines; they aren't meant to be machines. We're human beings, and almost everything about us is cyclical—even our work performance.

So, though that team tried, they couldn't sustain the ultra-consistency they were striving for. Despite their allegiance to the mistruth of "the same every day, come hell or high water!" their work energy and performance clearly displayed the ramp-up, the plateau, the downturn, and the low point I had observed in Josh and myself.

What I also saw was that this team's cycle was actually pretty short (much shorter than the other team I was charting—we'll get there). They ramped up quickly and attained their plateau but could only stay there for three or four days, not the two weeks I'd observed previously. After their brief time at apex performance, there was this tendency toward idleness, on a long downturn which led to a pretty substantial flatline.

I believe their devotion to consistency robbed them of their zeal to excel. If every day looked the same, where were the victories? Where were the season and offseason? What championship were they aiming for in the first place?

But that team's Performance Flow wasn't their fault; they'd been taught this "path of forced consistency" by their current employer and probably a few previous ones as well. The thing is, it was simply not a sustainable model. They would go up a little bit, achieve a little plateau, and then drop big. And the cycle would repeat.

Now onto the other team—and they weren't perfect either. Neither was I, but if the first team's goal was consistency, the second team's aim was *blitzkrieg*. They were go-go-go all the time. They wanted work. They wanted tickets. They wanted to get out in the field and make plays. So, they came in like gangbusters and went all gung-ho. Their ramp-up was a sharp-angled line up the graph. They truly could do great things.

But it was very obviously–in a different but related way to the other team's "consistency at all costs path"–unsustainable. It was almost as if this team got drunk off their work, binged for a while, and then fell over to sleep it off.

I knew we had some work ahead of us. I knew we could be better.

So, I had a long night with pen and paper and charts and data and all my nerdy things and came to the conclusion that I had to figure out a way to get both teams onto the same cycle. "Two teams, one Performance Flow," I said to myself. "That must be the answer!"

I maneuvered some things around and devised a way to get both teams on the same energy at the same time. I thought it was going to work. I *knew* it was going to work.

I was excited to see my hypothesis be proven correct.

It wasn't.

When I tried to put both teams on the same cycle, production levels plummeted.

It was the first setback to my little theory. I was like, "Why did that happen?" But I remembered Edison—and him first finding those 999 ways to make a lightbulb that didn't work.

I got more curious. More notes, more charts, more data. Then, at the end of another all-nighter, I decided to try the equal-and-opposite approach: I tried to get the two teams on the completely *opposite* cycle.

If we could achieve this, I thought, it would be balanced; when one team was on its way down, the other would be on its way up.

All I had to do was identify who was at the top of their game and who wasn't—and then assign work in such a way as to maximize the output. If I could pull it off, one team would always be at the top of their game! When the productivity of Team One began to wane, I could then call upon Team Two to pick up the slack.

Then, when the cycles flip-flopped, out of the bullpen like Mariano Rivera would come Team Two to relieve Team One.

We made the change, and the days went by. The days turned to weeks, and I started to see it work! I was thrilled. The teams were complimenting each other, almost symbiotic in their Performance Flows. It was the Ying/Yang in real life. I could see it clear as day—our productivity and mood had never been better.

I started telling members of my teams, "I don't care about you being individually consistent—but when you can go hard, go hard. Then, when you need to take a break, take a break."

I encouraged each team member to get an intimate knowledge of their personal Performance Flow, being aware that it is a real thing—as real as the cycle of the moon—so that it can be used for benefit.

"Do your work and achieve great things," I told them. "Go hard and long during your ramp-up and plateau, and then when you start your downturn, accept it; keep the vitals going, but rest your body and mind."

"Okay," they'd say, their eyes wanting to believe me, but all that conditioning made my words sound a little weird.

"And when you get to your bottom, take your day where you don't leave the house or when you go fishing or otherwise rejuvenate. And then come back strong."

Even as I said these words to my team, this concept was still hard for *me* to accept. Despite what I was observing and learning, it was still difficult for me to instill my own teachings. I had always been a guy who would push, push, push. It took a long time for me to wake up from the blindness and create my long-term schedule through six-week building blocks.

The more I have studied, observed, and worked with human beings in the workplace, the more I have found that this roughly six-week cycle pertains to almost all of us (and, yes, it should be taken into account when defining your season). Ideally, we would all play a six-week work schedule, take some time off, and then start up a new season. We all know it can't play out this cleanly all the time, but at least taking the concept into account when creating your schedules and projects goes a long way. It doesn't matter if you are working on a six-month project or a thirty-year project. Like the river flowing into the sea, that goal will be attained in a cyclic path (ever seen water flow? In nature, it never runs straight. It always meanders, and we are 70 percent water).

Indeed, "Everything straight lies. Life is crooked; time, itself, a cycle."

As a leader, be prepared to encourage or even challenge a team or individual when they are ramping up. Then, perhaps be a little bit more hands-off when they are nearing their low point. If you know which team or team members are on their way up–who is working at their highest plateau and who's about to be burnt out–you will instantly become a better leader.

If someone has a vacation coming up, they better have hit their plateau first. You don't want their potential best week at work in the past two months to be spent on a beach in Maui. Similarly, no teammate should leave for Acapulco during a ramp-up period. Conversely, no teammate should be slated to lead an important presentation on a Thursday three weeks from now when they will be at their low point in their Performance Flow.

To be the best leader you can be, maximize the Performance Flow of your team.

After a teammate has been treated like the cyclical-natured human being that they are and been allowed to rejuvenate, the vision is that they come back and hit the ground running. It's a Golden Rule thing: If I expect Dan to come back from his little offseason in great shape, I should expect myself to do the same.

This expectation from the workplace has always reminded me of baseball teams who employ five starting pitchers. This means that the starting pitcher, some of the best guys on the team, only plays one out of every five games. But when they are expected to go, they are expected to *really go*, to push themselves to the body/mind limit for the team.

Then, they are allotted the next four games off to ice the arm and prepare for their next start.

Some members of your team will be the stars, playing shortstop and hitting cleanup. Others will come in late in a game to provide some pep as a pinch hitter or pinch runner. There will be unforeseen scratches in the lineup, and people will have to step up. You'll have the one person on the team who knows how to keep the copy machine working like a wizard. Another teammate will be able to recruit like no one's business. You'll find contributions in myriad ways—especially when you optimize your team's Performance Flow.

Which we all can do.

Breaks and Self-Empathy

I have a friend named Sandra, who is a single mom. She's also a heck of an entrepreneur, and she works hard. Perhaps too hard.

Without work-life boundaries, Sandra admits that she would probably grind herself into dust.

Luckily, she has a built-in failsafe to guarantee that she does not burn out on her work; one week, her son is away at his father's, and one week he is with Sandra. During her son's absence, Sandra logs one hundred-plus hours of work. The next week, spent with her son, she's lucky to get twenty-five (I've seen her calendar, and the variance between weeks is huge—one is a multi-colored collage of meetings and deadlines, and the next week pretty much just says, "Harry.")

Although Sandra's cycle is almost compressed into these one-week spurts, she acknowledges that she also goes through the same long-term performance cycle. Interestingly, hers is not the six-week length I observe most often in human beings but more of a ninety-day cycle (twice the length, perhaps because she gets the alternating lighter work weeks peppered into her schedule). After about three months of amping up and plateauing, Sandra knows that it's time to take a full week off and go camping with Harry. She won't check her email for four to five days and only responds to her texts and calls on her own time.

Then she comes home and ramps up again.

Giving ourselves a break (just like when leadership gives its team a break) shows an element of self-empathy. Breaks–summer break, fall break, winter break–were part of our school year growing up. That's one thing that school gets right; that's why I believe that these types of breaks should be part of the work year when we grow up.

Breaks should be a part of our work because we live in a culture that praises long hours. We live in a culture that glorifies "the grind." The number of hours we Americans work has gone up considerably since the days of the Eisenhower administration. Americans work more hours today than we ever have. To take on this issue is another book altogether—I will simply say that by forgiving ourselves for not being able to keep an ultra-consistent schedule, we finally free ourselves to become more productive.

Still, it goes against so much of what we have been taught that it is hard to do. I had a brother-in-law coming over one weekend not too long ago, and I knew it was going to be awesome. We were going to go out to dinner and see both his daughter and granddaughter. We were going to have a lot of fun, and I was looking forward to it. But, on some level, I was also fighting it.

"I have to work," I kept telling myself. "I have all these to-dos that I have to cross off before Wayne gets here."

But nothing was getting done.

Then I looked at my Performance Flow schedule. I realized I was five-and-a-half weeks into my cycle. I was at the end of my Performance Flow. So, I figured I could forgive myself for a couple of days and just let go and start looking forward to the weekend with my family.

And I was grateful that my workplace allowed me to do that.

For me personally, I manipulate my schedule to maximize my daily work based on my large-scale schedule. Like with that vacation or with that very important event, I like to look at future dates of importance and then massage my Flow Performance to fit the task. If I know I have the most important day of my year on June 23; I will make sure that I get some rest about a three-weeks beforehand. That way, when the day comes, I will have ramped up and know I will be working at my highest plateau, both physically and mentally.

For instance, I started thinking about what I wanted to do *this week* a long time ago. I know I have a presentation to the city council on Thursday. It was a big week, for sure, but I had known about it for a while and had prepared to be at my peak Performance Flow to get the job done right.

Next week, after I'd hopefully nailed the presentation, I would start to taper off, and that's fine with my team and me.

It works well for all of us, and I encourage the leaders with whom I work to incorporate similar tactics. If you want to be a great leader, become aware of your Performance Cycle first, and then start to become aware of every individual on your team—and the team as a whole. Some individuals and teams will push steeper and faster. Others will go more gradually but for longer stretches. Yet all of us, no matter what our cycle looks like, experience one. Understanding this truth will make you a better leader right now.

The Eighth Key
Planning for the Future

We've focused on planning out your schedule to highlight key seasonal and game-like goals. This key will now bring us into some macro long-term foresight.

Though just about every spirituality book out there tells us to live in the present, we humans need things to look forward to. Perhaps it's some flaw in us; perhaps it's why we've come so far as a species. I am not sure; I just know that everyone, no matter what we are good at, likes to have things on the calendar to look forward to. What's coming up next? What are the exciting projects to look forward to? What are the fun things that I will get to do?

When infused into the workplace, this type of planning really starts to create a positive energy that is long-lasting and sustainable.

I'll go back to my friend, Sandra, the camper and rock climber you just learned about. Her excursions feed her soul—

and she peppers in these trips to the backcountry and to her local climbing spots throughout her long-term macro schedule. She usually plans them out about three months ahead of time.

Sandra's camping/climbing excursions fit well with what I've observed about us human beings at large; I've observed that both individuals and teams function better when we plan ninety days out. If you are a leader, you are essentially like a teacher back in high school; you don't need to know everything you are going to teach for the whole year, but your lesson plans *should* be scheduled in advance. You should know what the days will look like for you and your team ahead of time. Whether you are in education, maintenance, fashion design, or ice cream delivery, you better know, right now, what you are going to be achieving in ninety days.

Why ninety days? Well, it's long enough to plan for but still short enough to see the details. The flow of life and team are sharper in the ninety-day window. The focus is neither too distant nor too in your face. If you push it out much further, you risk having the amount of time become overwhelming and things getting vague. If you cram your foresight into only one-month increments, you won't have enough perspective. That is why I've found the ninety-day time frame for planning ahead, for how our minds work, helps us achieve more and better.

But just because ninety days fits pretty well with the quarterly calendar, don't feel obligated to fit yours rigidly to it. Plan your ninety-day bursts to maximize the performance of your unique team.

Plus, a few ninety-day plans put together create stout one- and five-year plans as well. They really do.

While we human beings are in our "today," we need to be thinking about our "tomorrow." It's not rocket science, but I find that a lot of the obvious things we do for our life, like planning for the future, just don't get absorbed by leadership in workplaces. That's why it is one of my keys to a healthy and thriving team. Good leaders are able to anticipate what things are going to look (and feel like) in three months—and then work to be prepared when that time comes.

Back in my maintenance days, I did not wait to think about that snow and ice until the first storm was upon us; no, I started to think about snow and ice in the heat of the summer when it was muggy out. I would look up at the hot blue sky and think about the wind chill and atmospheric rivers. And in ninety days, I would see this look in everybody's eyes like, "Wow, how are we so far ahead?"

Because we planned ahead.

This leads me to a key part of planning ahead: Planning celebrations.

I have found that healthy and successful workplaces plan celebrations, large and small, within their long-term macro schedule.

We human beings need to celebrate. We need to have that sense of accomplishment, feel that praise, and get those awards. After a job, a season, or an increment is completed, we

149

function better if we are recognized for it; at the end of each season, a celebration is in order.

A day of pizza and ice cream goes a long way after a long stretch of hard work. Plan them. A big bash at the end of the season can and will rejuvenate the team for the next season. Plan it now.

And celebrations can even be pretty micro, too; I've told you what a big "to-do list" person I am. Well, when I cross an item off of one of those lists, it's a little celebration every time. I plan it out; I get out my highlighter and strike it through that line—and it gives me a little dopamine rush every time.

These micro celebrations can get us through a day: Nine a.m., I accomplish something on my to-do list, and the highlighter comes out. Then again at 9:45. Then again an hour or so later, little celebrations throughout the day coming to lift me up and keep me going.

But still, I know that if I keep checking things off a list, I am not truly celebrating what I actually accomplished. After a while, a checklist *is just* a checklist. We human beings need more than that. We need emotions to be tied into our work. We need that Steve Eruzione moment—we need to celebrate the event with our team, sometimes in big ways.

Even if we have never put on an athletic uniform, we all have an innate craving, a desire, and a need to feel the exaltation of a win. We need the party at the end of the championship run.

Therefore, to optimize their team's purpose, vision and connectedness, I encourage every leader of every team to implement celebrations into their long-term macro scheduling. Every leader needs to give their team positive and reaffirming emotional moments, things that can be both looked forward to in anticipation and then looked back upon in joy.

I had a friend who used to be a ski bum. He got a job at a small mountain inn and restaurant right at the base of a big Lake Tahoe area ski resort. With a master's degree, he was way overqualified for the job, but most of his teammates were too. They knew they were taking this job as a means to live a unique life up in the mountains. The pay at the inn wasn't great, but there were other tangible incentives. The free ski season pass was one; meeting people from all over the world was one—and the team parties at the beginning and end of each season were one. The team at the inn would grind, work hard, extending themselves to help their guests enjoy their (very expensive) trip to the mountains. It was a small team, and they had to deal with the hellacious storms that ripped into the Sierra Nevada. A bartender could be out driving the snowplow. The GM may be up on the roof clearing the satellite dish from the two-foot snow drift that was blocking the signal and preventing the Olympics from airing.

But the team was tight. They were friends. They all gave a lot of themselves to make that old inn great, so it stayed open, and they could keep skiing every day and loving their mountain living.

During the grind of deep winter, my friend tells me, the team at the inn would talk about that spring shindig out at the pool in a couple of months. "It's going to be awesome!" they'd say. The free food, wine, games, and laughs were looked forward to all year (and the Christmas Party was usually a dance party worthy of a cover charge; people who didn't work at the inn would try to sneak in all the time to taste a little of the camaraderie).

Everything about those celebrations kept that little inn going—because it kept that little inn's *team* going.

Celebrations are not extraneous to a thriving workplace but a vital aspect of the workplace's plans for the future. Celebrations make people closer. They are a time to drink a little too much and a time to play a little too hard, a time to "be at work but not be working." For my friend, the old ski bum, those celebrations were one of the reasons he stayed at the inn for a couple of years longer than he thought he would. He, like all humans, had developed emotions about those celebrations that strengthened his resolve to work for and with his team.

Plus, leadership that celebrates well, I find, usually treats their team with great respect; this is because a celebration is a show of respect, a huge "thank you." All good leaders know they are void of purpose without people to lead—and celebrations go a long way to retaining and lifting up your team. I encourage you to use them.

Plan ahead. Build the ark before the rain; when you get where you want to go, put a plan in place to celebrate it.

It Starts with You

They say that there are around two hundred ways human beings communicate within the first fifteen seconds of interacting with someone. Truly, it is not always so much about what we are saying as about how we are saying it. As leaders, if we can cue into the human beings on our team and really get to know them, we can better inspire that person to find greatness. It is by listening and communicating and by being curious that we can help to celebrate the genius within them. In a large sense, a lot of what I encourage leaders to do is to talk less and listen more. This helps take potentially autocratic organizations and turn them into democratic teams. And, as I've hoped to show in this book, when we human beings work together, we all really do achieve more.

The best teams are those that are Human-Centered. The best teams give purpose, fulfillment, and joy to the humans that comprise them. The best teams are able to simply be themselves. The best teams are celebrated for who they are and for what they do.

Incorporating elements of the Workplace Pillars and Keys, I know from experience, helps teams, organizations, and businesses become their best. Just like with building a civilization, we must form our culture first. We build the structures, systems, and processes that keep it going. We create vision. We plan our seasons and get to know what victories look like—and then we celebrate them and keep going.

I went for a walk this morning. It was another beautiful day's dawn, and as I do, I got to thinking. I got to thinking about the word "optimism." I have mixed feelings about the word; sure, it has a positive connotation in our lexicon, but I feel the word and its meaning can and do leave too much to chance. Optimism can be a figment. Optimism can be fleeting. What truly moves human beings to move mountains, my experience has taught me, is belief.

What makes the future better is not optimism about it being better but a *firm belief* in it being better—and I firmly believe in the power of the Human-Centered workplace to help get us there.

I believe that the shift from profit to person, from cog to being, from employee to teammate, is the path forward for our organizations and our world.

True success in your organization comes from the belief

that one person has in the other people on the team. When we know someone has our back, we innately will have theirs. This instills the "together, we can do this" belief that wins championships.

Great workplaces are places where people know they are cared for. Great workplaces are places where excellence and innovation show up unabated and empowered. Great workplaces are infused with curiosity and laughter. Great workplaces are places where every human being can be themselves, places where the purpose is vision, and the vision is purpose.

Great workplaces put the human being first.

We can change the world by building Human-Centered Teams. I steadfastly believe this. There is a movement afoot in this vein, and I hope to continue to lead it from the front.

So, to close, I say, "Join us." Join the Human-Centered Movement—and see how far your team can go!

Acknowledgments

For as long as I can remember, I've read the acknowledgments of every book I've read. As I wrote this book, I finally realized why. It's because this section is always about the Team. No one takes on anything like this without a great team, and I had a world-class one for this project.

So many people showed up to align their vision and purpose with mine in this book.

I first want to acknowledge every person I have worked alongside in my career. There are too many of you to mention, but I am forever grateful for the lessons I learned from you. Thank You

Carrianne and Sarah (my first social media team)—you both got it from the beginning and jumped in with both feet. It has been an honor to watch my dream come to life through your eyes.

Stephanie Pierucci, Julie, Dale, and the Pierucci Publishing team. You promised a quick process, and I messed that up right away. You all were so patient and incredibly knowledgeable. Your process is as good as you are human beings. I hope I get to work with you all again!

Jonathan, we connected almost immediately, and I appreciate your dedication to getting this project right. Nothing worth it is ever easy. Thank you.

Dan—thank you for your honest feedback, coaching, and support in this project and in life. You have always seen the value in the movement, and I thank you for defending it as much as I do!

To my brothers Bob and Jim. We were raised together and are as different as any brothers I know. You are both an honor to our parents, and you both continue to honor them with your journey. I could not have chosen better brothers to have.

Ashley, you are an amazing person. Your work ethic, drive to serve others, and perseverance is the personification of this book. I am so proud to be your dad.

Josh, you have been on this journey for most of your life. For many years it was just "me and you against the world." You witnessed the formation and foundation of the movement. You have become the leader you were destined to be.

This project is nothing without the woman who has been alongside me for the last 25 years. Shari, you have seen the worst times of this journey, and you are still here! I am so grateful that you choose to love me. I can never express my love enough. I still owe you a few months of that great year!

We're Publishing!

Are you a mindful founder, CEO, entrepreneur, coach, or
healer looking to contribute your wisdom
to the great awakening?

Pierucci Publishing is your partner for creating and
marketing books that elevate world consciousness.

Please find us at www.PierucciPublishing.com to apply.

With love,

CEO, Pierucci Publishing
www.PierucciPublishing.com